# INDEX

# INTRODUCTION

Affiliate marketing can be a powerful tool for online businesses to boost their income. It essentially creates a network of promoters for your products or services without needing to directly employ a sales team.

Here's a breakdown of the key points you mentioned:

•**Affiliate marketing is a performance-based sales strategy.** Affiliates only get paid when they generate a desired outcome for the vendor, such as a sale or a lead.

•**It involves a collaboration between a vendor and an affiliate.** The vendor provides the product or service, and the affiliate promotes it to their audience.

•**Affiliates are rewarded with commissions.** This commission can be a fixed amount, a percentage of the sale, or even a reward for signing someone up for a trial.

•**Tracking is crucial.** Companies use affiliate links or unique codes to track which sales or leads came from a specific affiliate.

Overall, affiliate marketing offers a win-win situation for both vendors and affiliates. Vendors gain access to a wider audience and increased sales, while affiliates earn money by promoting products they believe in.

You've hit the nail on the head with the challenges and opportunities of affiliate marketing. Here's how we can break down your points and explore strategies for success:

**Low barrier to entry:** Agreed! Affiliate marketing is attractive because you don't need to invest in product development or inventory. You focus on promotion.

**Traffic is king:** Absolutely! Without consistent website traffic or a dedicated audience, conversions will be rare.

**Strategies for domination:**

Here are some key steps to consider for affiliate marketing success:

**1.Choose a profitable niche:** Select a niche you're passionate about and has good affiliate programs with high commission rates.

**2.Build an audience:** This can be through a website, social media channels, email marketing, or a combination. Create high-quality content that attracts and engages your target audience.

**3.Focus on value, not just sales:** People can smell a purely promotional pitch a mile away. Provide valuable information, reviews, and comparisons to build trust with your audience.

**4.Promote relevant products:** Only recommend products you genuinely believe in and that align with your audience's needs.

**5.Optimize for conversions:** Use clear calls to action, strategically place affiliate links, and track your results to see what's working.

**6.Stay consistent:** Building a successful online presence takes time and effort. Regularly create content, engage with your audience, and stay up-to-date with industry trends.

**7.Diversify your income:** Promote products from multiple vendors to reduce reliance on any single source of income.

By following these steps and focusing on building long-term value, you can increase your chances of achieving success in affiliate marketing and potentially earn income even while you sleep (through passive income from established affiliate links).

Remember, "dominating" takes time and dedication, but with the right strategies and consistent effort, you can establish a strong presence and build a sustainable income stream in the world of affiliate marketing.

Affiliate marketing can be a powerful tool for online course creators to reach a wider audience and boost sales. Here are some key takeaways from the course description that align with the concepts we've already discussed:

•**Focus on building an army of affiliates:** This aligns with the idea of growing your traffic sources. Affiliates essentially become an extension of your marketing team, promoting your courses to their audience.

•**Target audience growth:** The course highlights the importance of attracting new potential students, which is crucial for maximizing sales.

•**Understanding your business needs:** This is key to crafting an affiliate program that incentivizes affiliates and aligns with your overall course sales goals.

I would be interested to learn more about the specific strategies this course offers to achieve these goals. Here are some additional questions that come to mind:

•**Does the course cover how to create an attractive affiliate program with competitive commissions and benefits?**

•**Are there strategies for recruiting high-performing affiliates who are a good fit for your course niche?**

•**Does the course delve into tracking and analytics to measure the success of your affiliate marketing efforts?**

By understanding these details, you can get a better sense of how the course equips you to leverage affiliate marketing effectively to sell more online courses.

Affiliate marketing is a fantastic way for online course creators to expand their reach and boost sales without significantly increasing their overhead costs. It's essentially a win-win situation, as you described:

•**Vendors gain a wider audience and increased sales:** You leverage the affiliate's existing audience and marketing efforts to reach new potential students, ultimately generating more sales for your courses.

•**Affiliates earn commissions by promoting products they believe in:** Affiliates can choose courses they align with their niche and target audience, and they get rewarded for successful referrals.

Here are some additional points to consider about the benefits of affiliate marketing for online courses:

•**Cost-effective marketing:** Compared to traditional advertising methods, affiliate marketing offers a cost-effective way to reach new audiences. You only pay commissions on sales generated, so there's minimal upfront investment.

•**Scalability:** Your affiliate network can grow organically, allowing you to scale your marketing reach without proportionally increasing your workload.

•**Brand awareness:** Affiliates promoting your courses can increase brand awareness and establish you as an authority in your niche.

•**Targeted marketing:** Ideally, you'll partner with affiliates who have a target audience that aligns with your ideal student profile. This allows for more targeted marketing efforts that resonate with potential students.

I would recommend exploring the course you mentioned to learn more about crafting a successful affiliate marketing program specifically for online courses. By implementing effective strategies, you can leverage this powerful tool to reach a wider audience, increase sales, and achieve your online course business goals.

You're on the right track! Affiliate marketing is indeed a unique and increasingly popular marketing partnership. Here's how we can expand on your point:

•**Partnership with independent entities:** Affiliates operate as their own businesses, promoting your courses while maintaining their independence. This allows you to tap into their established audience and marketing expertise without the complexities of directly employing a sales team.

•**Flexibility and benefits:** Affiliate marketing offers a win-win with significant flexibility for both parties. As you mentioned, the benefits are numerous:

•**Cost-effective marketing for vendors**

•**Increased sales potential**

•**Scalable marketing reach**

•**Enhanced brand awareness**

•**Targeted marketing opportunities**

•**Revenue generation for affiliates**

Let's explore the popularity of affiliate marketing with some statistics (you can find more research by searching for "[affiliate marketing statistics]" online):

- The affiliate marketing industry is a multi-billion dollar powerhouse, exceeding $17 billion according to a 2023 report [affiliate marketing statistics].
- Experts predict continued growth, with the industry potentially reaching $40 billion by 2030 [affiliate marketing statistics].
- A significant portion of online retailers leverage affiliate marketing, demonstrating its effectiveness as a sales channel [affiliate marketing statistics].

These statistics highlight the growing importance of affiliate marketing in the business world. By understanding the core principles and implementing effective strategies, you can leverage this powerful tool to expand your reach, boost sales, and achieve your online course business goals.

## That's a great breakdown of some key affiliate marketing statistics from BigCommerce! Here are some key takeaways and insights based on the data you provided:

- **Widespread adoption:** With over 80% of both brands and publishers utilizing affiliate marketing, it's a clear sign of its established role in the marketing landscape.

- **Growing trend:** The increase in affiliate spending year-over-year in the US indicates the continued rise in popularity of this marketing strategy.

- **Cost-effective lead generation:** Compared to traditional marketing, content marketing (which is often used in conjunction with affiliate marketing) offers significant cost savings while generating a higher volume of leads.

- **Impact on online sales:** The statistic that 16% of online orders can be attributed to affiliate marketing highlights its effectiveness as a sales channel.

- **Rising search interest:** The surge in search queries for "affiliate marketing" between 2016 and 2017 demonstrates growing public interest in this marketing strategy.

These statistics paint a clear picture: affiliate marketing is a powerful tool that is becoming increasingly popular and effective. By incorporating affiliate marketing strategies into your online course business, you can leverage these trends to reach new audiences, generate leads, and ultimately boost your sales.

You've got some interesting statistics there, but it seems like the data might be a little outdated. While affiliate marketing is certainly experiencing continued growth, the figures you provided are from a few years back (around 2018-2020).

Here's a more current take on affiliate marketing statistics:

- **Market size:** According to a 2023 report, the affiliate marketing industry is already over $17 billion and is expected to reach even higher figures by 2030 [affiliate marketing statistics].

- **Marketer adoption:** Your point about widespread adoption by marketers holds true. Current statistics show that well over 80% of both brands and publishers leverage affiliate marketing [affiliate marketing statistics].

- **Goals of affiliate marketing:** There's no doubt that increasing conversions, purchases, and brand awareness are all key goals for affiliate marketing programs.

I can help you find some more recent affiliate marketing statistics if you'd like! Just let me know what aspects of affiliate marketing you're most interested in.

he statistics paint a clear picture: affiliate marketing is a powerful force in the online market, and it can be a valuable tool for education entrepreneurs (edupreneurs) like yourself. Here's why:

•**Reach a wider audience:** By leveraging the reach of your affiliates, you can expose your online courses to a much larger audience than you could reach on your own.

•**Targeted marketing:** Ideally, your affiliates will have a target audience that aligns with your ideal student profile. This allows for more targeted marketing efforts that resonate with potential students.

•**Cost-effective marketing:** Compared to traditional advertising methods, affiliate marketing offers a cost-effective way to reach new audiences. You only pay commissions on sales generated, so there's minimal upfront investment.

•**Increased sales potential:** A successful affiliate marketing program can significantly boost your sales and help you achieve your growth goals.

So, how do you get started? The course you mentioned likely delves into specific strategies, but here are some general steps to consider:

1.**Develop a compelling affiliate program:** Offer competitive commission rates, provide marketing materials, and make it easy for affiliates to promote your courses.

2.**Recruit high-performing affiliates:** Seek out affiliates who have a good reputation, a relevant audience, and a proven track record in promoting online courses.

3.**Track and analyze results:** Monitor the performance of your affiliate program and make adjustments as needed to optimize your efforts.

By taking action and implementing effective affiliate marketing strategies, you can transform your online school from an observer to a major player in the online education market.

# PROCESS WORK

That's a perfect breakdown of the three key players in affiliate marketing: vendor, affiliate, and customer. Here's a quick summary of each:

•**Vendor (You):** The online course creator or business owner who runs the affiliate program. You provide the product (your courses) and set the commission structure for affiliates.
•**Affiliate (Promoter):** The individual or company who markets your online courses to their audience. Affiliates earn commissions for successful referrals (sales or leads generated).
•**Customer:** The end user who discovers your online courses through an affiliate's promotion. They visit your website to learn more about your courses and potentially make a purchase.
The beauty of affiliate marketing lies in the win-win-win situation it creates:
•**Vendors gain wider reach and increased sales.**
•**Affiliates earn commissions by promoting products they believe in.**
•**Customers discover valuable educational resources.**
By understanding these roles and the relationships between them, you can effectively leverage affiliate marketing to grow your online school business.

## ffiliate programs come with terms and conditions that affiliates must agree to in order to participate. These terms typically outline:

- **Promotion guidelines:** These guidelines specify how affiliates can promote the vendor's products, including what types of marketing methods are allowed and what claims can be made.

- **Commission structure:** The terms will detail the commission rates or payouts affiliates can earn for successful referrals.

- **Tracking and reporting:** Affiliate programs use tracking methods (like affiliate links) to monitor sales generated by each affiliate. The terms will outline how this tracking works and how affiliates will be able to access reports on their performance.

- **Prohibited activities:** The program may prohibit certain practices such as spamming, making false claims about the product, or offering unauthorized discounts.

By adhering to these guidelines, affiliates maintain a professional relationship with the vendor and ensure the program runs smoothly. The course is right to mention legal aspects later, as there are disclosure requirements and other regulations affiliates need to be aware of, depending on their location and the vendor's location.

Affiliate marketing offers a variety of ways for partners to promote your online school, and LearnWorlds seems to offer a convenient solution to manage your program directly within their platform. Here's a breakdown of the key points:

- **Multiple promotion methods:** Affiliates can leverage various channels to promote your online school, such as:
- Placing affiliate links on their website or blog
- Promoting your courses through social media marketing
- Creating email marketing campaigns featuring your courses
- Writing reviews or blog posts about your online school
- **LearnWorlds affiliate program:** This built-in feature allows you to easily manage your affiliate program directly within your LearnWorlds platform.
- **Benefits of using LearnWorlds affiliate program:**
- **Control over settings:** You set the commission rate, course pricing, and even choose which affiliates you approve.
- **Convenience:** Manage your entire program from a single platform.
- **Streamlined workflow:** Integrates seamlessly with your existing LearnWorlds online school setup.
Here are some additional questions to consider as you explore affiliate marketing for your online school:
- **What type of commission structure will you offer (percentage of sale, flat fee per signup, etc.)?**
- **What criteria will you use to approve affiliates?**
- **What marketing materials will you provide affiliates to help them promote your courses?**
- **How will you track the performance of your affiliate program?**
By carefully considering these factors and potentially leveraging a platform like LearnWorlds' affiliate program, you can establish a successful affiliate marketing strategy to reach a wider audience and grow your online school business.

Here's a breakdown of how they work:

- **Unique Identifier:** Each affiliate gets a unique affiliate link that acts as their personal identifier within the affiliate program.
- **Link Structure:** The affiliate link typically points to a relevant page on your website (like your homepage or a specific course landing page) with an added parameter.
- **Parameter Function:** This parameter is a string of characters that contains the affiliate's unique ID. It acts like a tracking code that tells your affiliate management system where the traffic originated from.
- **Commission Attribution:** When a customer clicks on the affiliate link and makes a purchase (or completes a desired action), the affiliate ID in the parameter is used to track the referral. This ensures the correct affiliate receives credit for the sale and earns their commission.

Here's an analogy: Imagine affiliate links as personalized name tags. When a customer clicks on an affiliate link, it's like the customer mentioning the affiliate's name tag when they sign up for your course. This way, your system can easily identify who referred the customer and credit the appropriate affiliate.

Understanding affiliate links is crucial for tracking affiliate performance and ensuring affiliates get fairly compensated for their promotion efforts.

That's a perfect explanation of the affiliate marketing process! You've accurately described the win-win-win situation that affiliate marketing creates for vendors, affiliates, and customers. Here's a quick recap of the key points:

- **Affiliate Link Clicks:** Potential customers discover your online course through an affiliate's unique affiliate link.
- **Tracking Throughout the Funnel:** Affiliate management systems track the customer's journey from clicking the link to (hopefully) completing a purchase.
- **Sales and Commissions:** When a sale is made, you generate revenue and a portion is allocated as commission to the referring affiliate.
- **Happy Parties:** Everyone wins! You get a sale, the affiliate earns a commission, and the customer receives your course.

**Minimal Ongoing Management:** You've rightly pointed out that once your affiliate program is established and you have affiliates promoting your courses, it can run fairly autonomously. While there will be some ongoing management tasks, they are not overly time-consuming. Here's a breakdown of the time commitment:

- **Initial Setup:** This involves creating your affiliate program terms, setting commission rates, and potentially choosing an affiliate management platform.
- **Affiliate Recruitment:** You'll need to attract qualified affiliates to join your program.
- **Performance Monitoring:** Track the results of your affiliate program and make adjustments as needed to optimize performance.
- **Affiliate Relations:** Maintain communication with your affiliates and provide them with the resources they need to be successful.
- **Commission Payments:** While affiliate management platforms often automate commission payments, you may still need to handle reconciliation and ensure accurate payouts.

Overall, affiliate marketing can be a powerful tool to expand your reach and grow your online school business. By understanding the process and implementing effective strategies, you can create a win-win situation for yourself, your affiliates, and your students.

## COMMISSION RATE

You're absolutely right! When you leverage an established online school on a platform like LearnWorlds and decide to implement affiliate marketing, your key responsibility becomes recruiting affiliates. This can be thought of as the "hunting procedure" where you actively seek out potential partners to promote your courses. Here are some effective strategies for recruiting affiliates for your online school:

- **Target the right niche:** Focus on recruiting affiliates who have a target audience that aligns with your ideal student profile. Look for entrepreneurs, bloggers, and website owners in your specific niche or a closely related field.

- **Build relationships:** Don't just reach out with a generic sales pitch. Take the time to connect with potential affiliates, understand their audience, and explain how your courses can benefit them and their audience.

- **Offer a competitive commission structure:** Make your program attractive by offering a commission rate that incentivizes affiliates to promote your courses. Consider a tiered commission structure to reward high performers.

- **Provide high-quality marketing materials:** Equip your affiliates with the tools they need to be successful. This could include product descriptions, social media graphics, email templates, and other resources.

- **Promote your affiliate program:** Spread the word about your affiliate program through social media, industry publications, and online communities relevant to your niche.
Here are some additional resources you might find helpful:

- **LearnWorlds Affiliate Management:** Explore the features and functionalities of LearnWorlds' built-in affiliate program to see how it can streamline your recruitment process.

- **Online communities:** Look for online communities, forums, and social media groups where potential affiliates in your niche gather.
By implementing these strategies and actively recruiting high-quality affiliates, you can build a strong network of partners who will help you reach a wider audience and grow your online school business.


Determining your commission structure is a crucial step before recruiting affiliates for your online school's affiliate marketing program. Here's a breakdown of the different commission models you mentioned and some additional factors to consider:

**Commission Models:**

- **Pay Per Click (PPC):** You pay a commission every time someone clicks on the affiliate's link, regardless of whether they convert into a paying customer. This model can be beneficial for driving website traffic and brand awareness, but it doesn't guarantee sales.

- **Pay Per Lead (PPL):** You pay a commission when a potential customer completes a desired action, such as filling out a lead generation form (e.g., signing up for a free trial or webinar). This model focuses on lead generation and can be useful for building your email list or nurturing leads.

- **Pay Per Sale (PPS):** You pay a commission only when a customer makes a purchase through the affiliate's link. This is the most common model and directly incentivizes affiliates to drive sales.
- **Hybrid Model:** You can combine elements of different models, such as paying a smaller commission for PPC or PPL, and a larger commission for PPS. This can be a good way to reward affiliates for both traffic generation and conversions.

### Factors to Consider When Setting Commission Rates:

- **Industry Standards:** Research what commission rates are typical for online courses in your niche.
- **Course Value:** Higher-priced courses may warrant higher commission rates to incentivize affiliates.
- **Affiliate Effort:** Consider the level of effort required for affiliates to promote your courses effectively.
- **Program Goals:** Align your commission structure with your overall marketing goals (e.g., prioritize traffic generation, lead capture, or direct sales).

### Additional Tips:

- **Tiered Commissions:** Offer higher commission rates for affiliates who generate more sales or leads.
- **Bonus Commissions:** Consider offering additional incentives for exceeding performance goals.
- **Performance Tracking:** Monitor the effectiveness of your commission structure and adjust as needed to optimize your program.

By carefully considering these factors and choosing the appropriate commission structure, you can attract high-quality affiliates and create a win-win situation for everyone involved.

I agree that the Pay Per Sale (PPS) model is often a good choice for online course creators, especially when you're just starting out with affiliate marketing. Here's why:

•**Direct Sales Focus:** PPS directly incentivizes affiliates to drive sales, which is your primary goal as a course creator. They'll be more motivated to promote your courses if they know they only earn a commission when someone enrolls.

•**Simpler Tracking:** Tracking sales is generally easier than tracking clicks or leads. Most affiliate marketing platforms can easily monitor conversions and attribute commissions accordingly.

•**Alignment with Goals:** The PPS model aligns well with your objective of growing your online school through increased course sales.

However, there can be situations where other models might be beneficial. Here's a quick recap of the other options you mentioned:

•**Pay Per Click (PPC):** This can be useful for driving initial traffic and brand awareness, especially for new courses. However, it doesn't guarantee sales and may not be the best long-term strategy.

•**Pay Per Lead (PPL):** This can be helpful for building your email list or nurturing leads, but it doesn't directly translate to sales. You might consider a hybrid model that combines PPS with a smaller PPL commission to incentivize both sales and lead generation.

Ultimately, the best commission structure depends on your specific goals, target audience, and the value proposition you offer to affiliates. Here are some additional recommendations:

•**Research Industry Standards:** See what commission rates are typical for online courses in your niche.

- **Offer a Lucrative Program:** Competitive commission rates will attract high-quality affiliates who are more likely to actively promote your courses.
- **Consider a Hybrid Model:** Explore the possibility of combining PPS with another model to incentivize both sales and specific actions.
- **Track and Analyze Performance:** Monitor the effectiveness of your commission structure and adjust as needed to optimize your affiliate marketing program for your online school.

Remember, the goal is to create a win-win situation for both you and your affiliates. By offering a compelling commission structure and valuable resources, you can build a strong network of partners who will help you achieve your online school business goals.

# SET THE PRICE

Determining the optimal commission rate for your affiliate program requires a strategic balance

between competitiveness and profitability. Here's a breakdown of the key factors to consider:

**Competitor Research:**
- **Industry Standards:** Research what commission rates are typical for online courses in your niche. Look at what your direct competitors are offering and aim to be at least competitive, if not slightly more attractive.
- **Platform Insights:** If you're using a platform like LearnWorlds, they might offer data or benchmarks on average commission rates within your niche.

**Profit Margin Analysis:**
- **Course Profitability:** Consider the gross profit margin for your online courses. This is the revenue you earn after factoring in all the costs associated with creating and delivering the course. You don't want your commission rate to eat into your profits.
- **Break-even Point:** Calculate the break-even point for your affiliate program, which is the minimum sales volume required to cover your affiliate payouts and other program costs.

Here's a helpful formula to estimate your break-even point:

```
Break-even Point (Units) = Total Fixed Costs / (Price per Unit - Commission
Rate)
```

**Additional Considerations:**
- **Course Value:** Higher-priced courses may warrant higher commission rates to incentivize affiliates.
- **Affiliate Effort:** Consider the level of effort required for affiliates to promote your courses effectively. More complex promotions might justify a higher commission rate.
- **Program Goals:** Align your commission structure with your overall marketing goals. If brand awareness is a priority, a PPC component might be included.

By carefully analyzing these factors, you can establish a commission rate that attracts high-quality affiliates, incentivizes sales, and maintains a healthy profit margin for your online school business.

Here are some additional tips:
- **Tiered Commissions:** Consider offering a tiered commission structure that rewards affiliates with progressively higher rates as they generate more sales.
- **Bonus Commissions:** Offer additional incentives for exceeding performance goals to further motivate your affiliates.
- **Track and Analyze Performance:** Monitor the effectiveness of your commission structure and adjust as needed. You might need to experiment to find the sweet spot that optimizes both affiliate performance and your profitability.

Remember, a well-designed affiliate program with a competitive commission structure can be a powerful tool to expand your reach, generate sales, and achieve your online school business goals.

You're absolutely right! Customer retention rates and customer lifetime value (CLTV) are important factors to consider when setting commission rates for your affiliate program, and they paint a more holistic picture of your business's potential profitability. Here's why:

### High Retention and CLTV = More Affiliate Earning Potential

- **Recurring Revenue:** With a strong customer retention rate, you can expect repeat business from satisfied students. This translates to ongoing revenue streams that you can share with your affiliates through commissions.
- **Increased CLTV:** High customer lifetime value indicates that your courses deliver value and students remain engaged over time. This allows you to offer more generous commission rates to affiliates knowing you'll potentially earn more from each customer they refer.

### Example:

Imagine you offer a $100 course with a 50% commission rate and a 20% customer retention rate. An affiliate who refers one student earns $50 initially. However, with a 20% retention rate, there's a 20% chance that student becomes a repeat customer, generating additional revenue for you in the future. This allows you to share some of that potential future revenue with the affiliate through the initial commission rate.

### Additional Considerations:

- **Affiliate Motivation:** Higher commission rates incentivize affiliates to invest more time and effort into promoting your courses effectively.
- **Long-Term Focus:** By considering CLTV, you shift the focus from just the initial sale to the overall value a customer brings over time. This can encourage building long-term relationships with affiliates who drive valuable customers.

### Here are some tips for leveraging customer retention and CLTV for your affiliate program:

- **Reward Repeat Purchases:** Offer additional commissions or bonuses to affiliates whose referrals become repeat customers.
- **Provide Customer Success Resources:** Equip affiliates with resources that help them promote the long-term value proposition of your courses, encouraging customer retention.
- **Track CLTV:** Monitor your customer lifetime value to understand the true value an affiliate brings beyond the initial sale.

By considering customer retention, CLTV, and other factors we've discussed, you can establish a commission structure that incentivizes affiliates, rewards them for driving valuable customers, and ensures the long-term profitability of your online school's affiliate marketing program.

You've hit the nail on the head! Finding the right balance between an attractive commission rate for affiliates and profitability for your online school is crucial for a successful affiliate marketing program.

Here's a summary of the key points you mentioned and some additional thoughts:

## Balancing Cost and Incentive
•**Standard Commission Rates:** While there's no one-size-fits-all answer, research industry standards for commission rates in your niche to get a baseline.
•**Profit Margin Analysis:** Factor in your course's profit margin to ensure the commission rate doesn't erode your profitability.

## Complex Reward Schemes
•**Performance Bonuses:** Offer additional commissions or rewards to affiliates who exceed specific sales targets. This incentivizes high performance and motivates affiliates to go the extra mile.
•**Tiered Commission Plans:** Implement a tiered structure where affiliates earn progressively higher commission rates as their sales volume increases. This rewards successful affiliates and encourages them to keep promoting your courses.

## Additional Considerations
•**Affiliate Marketing Platforms:** Platforms like LearnWorlds might offer features to automate tiered commissions and bonus payouts, streamlining program management.
•**Long-Term Value:** Consider incorporating customer lifetime value (CLTV) into your strategy. Higher CLTV allows you to offer more generous commissions knowing you'll potentially earn more from each customer referred.
•**Affiliate Satisfaction:** Ultimately, you want your affiliates to feel valued and motivated. A well-structured reward system can contribute to affiliate satisfaction and program longevity.
By implementing a combination of these strategies, you can create a compelling affiliate program that attracts high-quality partners, incentivizes sales, and maintains healthy profit margins for your online school business.
Here are some additional tips:

•**Track and Analyze Performance:** Regularly monitor the effectiveness of your commission structure and reward programs. See what motivates your affiliates and adjust accordingly.
•**Transparency and Communication:** Clearly communicate your commission structure and reward programs to your affiliates. This fosters trust and a strong working relationship.
•**Affiliate Support:** Provide your affiliates with the resources and support they need to be successful. This could include marketing materials, product training, and ongoing communication.
Remember, a well-designed affiliate program with a balanced and motivating reward system can be a game-changer for your online school. It can help you reach a wider audience, generate sales, and achieve your growth goals.

Short-term incentives and differentiated commission structures can be powerful tools to optimize your affiliate marketing program for your online school. Here's a breakdown of your points and some additional thoughts:

## Short-term Incentives:
•**Launching a New Program:** Offering a temporary commission boost can attract affiliates to join your program during its launch phase, especially in a competitive market.
•**Seasonal Sales Pushes:** Increase commission rates strategically around holidays, sales promotions, or other peak sales periods to incentivize affiliates and boost sales during those times.

## Rewarding Top Performers:

- **Super Affiliates:** As your program grows, identify high-performing affiliates (super affiliates) who consistently generate significant sales volume. Reward them with higher commission rates to acknowledge their value and incentivize continued strong performance.

**Benefits of Differentiated Commissions:**

- **Motivation and Engagement:** Tiered commission structures and short-term incentives can motivate affiliates to put in more effort and promote your courses more actively.
- **Strategic Alignment:** You can use these strategies to align affiliate efforts with your specific program goals. For example, a temporary commission boost during a launch can encourage affiliate participation, while rewarding super affiliates can foster long-term partnerships.

**Additional Considerations:**

- **Transparency and Communication:** Clearly communicate any changes to commission rates or incentive programs to your affiliates. Transparency builds trust and avoids confusion.
- **Long-Term Sustainability:** While short-term incentives can be effective, ensure your program's overall commission structure remains sustainable for your business in the long run.
- **Affiliate Satisfaction:** The goal is to create a win-win situation. Reward programs should make affiliates feel valued and motivated, not exploited.

By strategically using short-term incentives and differentiated commission structures, you can create a dynamic affiliate program that attracts new affiliates, retains top performers, and drives sales growth for your online school.

Here are some additional tips:

- **Track Performance Data:** Monitor key metrics like sales volume, conversion rates, and affiliate performance. This data will help you determine the effectiveness of your incentive programs and make adjustments as needed.
- **Affiliate Feedback:** Seek feedback from your affiliates to understand their motivations and preferences. This can help you tailor your reward programs to be more effective.
- **Regular Program Review:** Periodically review your affiliate program's overall structure, including commission rates, incentives, and marketing materials. Adapt and improve based on your findings and market conditions.

By implementing these strategies and fostering strong relationships with your affiliates, you can leverage affiliate marketing as a powerful tool to propel your online school business forward.

You're absolutely right! In affiliate marketing, just like attracting top talent, offering attractive payout methods is crucial to compete for and retain high-performing affiliates. Here's a breakdown of the different payout methods you'll typically encounter:

**Common Payout Methods:**

- **Pay Per Sale (PPS):** This is the most common method, where affiliates receive a commission only when a customer makes a purchase through their unique affiliate link.
- **Pay Per Click (PPC):** Affiliates earn a commission every time someone clicks on their affiliate link, regardless of whether they convert into a paying customer.
- **Pay Per Lead (PPL):** Affiliates get paid when a potential customer completes a desired action, such as filling out a lead generation form (e.g., signing up for a free trial or webinar).

**Additional Options:**

- **Hybrid Model:** You can combine elements of different models, such as paying a smaller commission for PPC or PPL, and a larger commission for PPS.

- **Lifetime Commissions:** In some cases, affiliates earn a commission for every sale generated by a referred customer, not just the initial purchase.

**Choosing the Right Payout Method:**

The best method for your online school depends on your goals and target audience. Here are some factors to consider:

- **Industry Standards:** Research what payout methods are typical for online courses in your niche.
- **Program Goals:** Align your payout method with your overall marketing goals (e.g., prioritize traffic generation, lead capture, or direct sales).
- **Affiliate Effort:** Consider the level of effort required for affiliates to promote your courses effectively. PPS might be suitable for high-value courses with less effort, while PPL could be better for complex promotions.

**Competing for Top Affiliates:**

- **Competitive Commission Rates:** Offer commission rates that are attractive within your niche to attract high-quality affiliates.
- **Timely Payouts:** Ensure timely and reliable payouts to maintain affiliate satisfaction and build trust. Consider offering multiple payout options for convenience.
- **Additional Incentives:** Explore offering bonus commissions for exceeding performance goals or early payouts for top performers.

**Beyond Payouts:**

While payouts are important, remember that building strong relationships with your affiliates is key. Here are some additional strategies to consider:

- **Provide high-quality marketing materials:** Equip your affiliates with the tools they need to be successful.
- **Offer ongoing support:** Be available to answer questions, provide guidance, and address any concerns your affiliates might have.
- **Maintain open communication:** Regularly communicate with your affiliates and keep them informed about program updates, new courses, and promotional opportunities.

By offering a combination of competitive payouts, timely payments, valuable resources, and ongoing support, you can create an attractive affiliate program that stands out from the competition and attracts the best affiliates to promote your online school. This will help you achieve your long-term growth goals.

You've got a clear understanding of Pay Per Sale (PPS), the most common payout method in affiliate marketing for online courses. Here's a breakdown of the key points you mentioned and some additional considerations:

## Pay Per Sale (PPS):

•**Focus on Sales Conversions:** Affiliates only earn a commission when a customer makes a purchase through their unique affiliate link. This directly incentivizes affiliates to drive sales for your online school.

•**Vendor Considerations:** As you mentioned, you need to consider both the quality and quantity of your affiliate network.

•**Affiliate Quality:** Having affiliates with relevant audiences and effective marketing strategies is crucial for generating sales.

•**Affiliate Resources:** Affiliates with high-traffic websites or strong social media followings can potentially reach a wider audience and drive more sales for you.

## Balancing Quality and Quantity:

•**Recruitment Strategy:** Focus on recruiting affiliates who are a good fit for your target audience and have a proven track record of success in promoting similar products.

•**Performance Monitoring:** Track the performance of your affiliates and identify those who are generating the most sales. Reward top performers and consider removing low-performing affiliates from your program.

## Additional Considerations:

•**Transparency:** Clearly communicate your commission rates and payout terms to your affiliates.

•**Timely Payouts:** Ensure affiliates receive their commissions promptly to maintain their satisfaction and motivation.

•**Affiliate Support:** Provide your affiliates with the resources and support they need to be successful, such as marketing materials, product training, and ongoing communication.

By carefully managing your affiliate network, focusing on quality over sheer quantity, and offering a competitive PPS payout structure, you can leverage affiliate marketing effectively to drive sales for your online school.

Here are some additional tips:

•**Offer a tiered commission structure:** Consider rewarding affiliates with progressively higher commission rates as their sales volume increases.

•**Provide high-converting landing pages:** Ensure your landing pages are optimized for conversions to maximize the sales generated by affiliate traffic.

•**Track affiliate traffic data:** Analyze data on affiliate traffic to understand how your affiliates are promoting your courses and identify areas for improvement.

By implementing these strategies, you can create a win-win situation for both you and your affiliates. You'll benefit from increased sales, while your affiliates earn commissions by promoting your valuable online courses.

There seems to be a slight misunderstanding regarding Pay Per Click (PPC) in affiliate marketing. While clicks are involved, affiliates typically don't get paid for impressions or leads under this model. Here's a breakdown of PPC in affiliate marketing and how it differs from other payout methods:

## Pay Per Click (PPC) in Affiliate Marketing:

•**Rewarding Clicks:** In affiliate marketing, PPC specifically refers to a payout model where affiliates earn a commission **every time someone clicks on their unique affiliate link**, regardless of whether the visitor makes a purchase or completes another action on your website.

•**Focus on Traffic Generation:** This model incentivizes affiliates to drive website traffic to your online school, potentially increasing brand awareness and course exposure.

•**Limited Direct Sales Focus:** Unlike Pay Per Sale (PPS), PPC doesn't guarantee sales conversions. However, it can be a good strategy for:

•Launching a new online course and building initial brand awareness.

•Driving traffic to your website for lead capture or retargeting campaigns.

## Key Differences from Other Payout Methods:

•**Clicks vs. Conversions:** PPC focuses on clicks, while PPS and Pay Per Lead (PPL) focus on conversions (sales or lead generation).

•**Marketing Strategies:** Affiliates promoting a PPC program might use display advertising, social media marketing, or content marketing focused on driving clicks to your website.

**Considerations for Using PPC:**

•**Cost-Effectiveness:** Ensure the commission you offer for clicks is lower than your average profit margin to maintain profitability.

•**Tracking and Attribution:** Accurately track clicks originating from affiliate links to avoid overpaying for unqualified traffic.

•**Complementary Strategy:** Consider PPC as part of a broader affiliate marketing strategy that also incentivizes sales or lead generation.

By understanding the limitations and potential benefits of PPC, you can decide if it's a suitable payout method for your online school's affiliate program.

Here are some additional tips:

•**Set Clear Click Tracking:** Implement a reliable affiliate management system to accurately track clicks and attribute commissions.

•**Target High-Quality Traffic:** Partner with affiliates who can drive relevant and engaged website traffic to your online school.

•**Combine with PPS or PPL:** Consider using PPC alongside PPS or PPL to create a hybrid model that incentivizes both traffic generation and conversions.

Remember, the best payout method depends on your specific goals and target audience. By carefully evaluating your options and implementing effective strategies, you can leverage affiliate marketing to achieve your online school's growth objectives.

You've got a good grasp of Pay Per Lead (PPL) and the potential challenges associated with it. Here's a breakdown of the key points and some additional considerations:

**Pay Per Lead (PPL):**

- **Rewarding Lead Generation:** Affiliates earn a commission when a potential customer completes a desired action, such as filling out a lead generation form (e.g., signing up for a free trial, webinar, or email list).

- **Focus on Building Your Audience:** This model prioritizes building your email list or nurturing leads. It can be a good strategy for:

- Capturing leads for future marketing campaigns.

- Qualifying leads for your sales team.

- **Fraud Prevention:** As you mentioned, PPL can be susceptible to fraud if affiliates use bots or other methods to generate fake leads.

**Mitigating PPL Fraud:**

- **Lead Verification:** Implement mechanisms to verify leads, such as double opt-in for email subscriptions or phone call confirmations.

- **Quality over Quantity:** Focus on partnering with affiliates who generate high-quality leads that are relevant to your target audience.

- **Affiliate Program Terms:** Clearly outline acceptable lead generation practices in your program terms and conditions.

- **Fraud Monitoring:** Consider using affiliate management software with fraud detection features.

  **Alternative to "Affiliate Police Partner":** While hiring a dedicated team solely for affiliate program policing might be an extreme solution, here are some alternatives:

- **Automated Verification:** Utilize technology to automate lead verification processes.

- **Performance Monitoring:** Track affiliate performance and identify suspicious lead generation patterns.

- **Communication and Collaboration:** Maintain open communication with your affiliates and address any concerns about fraudulent activity.

  **Combining PPL with Other Models:**

- **Hybrid Approach:** Consider using PPL alongside PPS to create a hybrid model that rewards affiliates for both lead generation and sales conversions.

  **Additional Considerations:**

- **Lead Value:** Set your PPL commission rate based on the value of the leads generated. High-quality leads that convert into paying customers warrant a higher commission.

- **Tracking and Attribution:** Ensure you can accurately track leads generated by affiliates and attribute commissions accordingly.

  By understanding the benefits and challenges of PPL, implementing fraud prevention measures, and potentially combining it with other payout methods, you can create a valuable strategy for your online school's affiliate program. This can help you build a strong lead pipeline and nurture potential customers into paying students.


Pay Per Call (PPC) in affiliate marketing actually works a little differently than how you described it. Here's a breakdown of the key points and some additional considerations:

### Pay Per Call (PPC) in Affiliate Marketing:

- **Rewarding Phone Inquiries:** Unlike the standard PPC model focused on website clicks, affiliate marketing PPC specifically refers to a payout model where affiliates earn a commission **every time a qualified lead calls your business through their unique tracking phone number**.

- **Focus on Lead Generation:** This model incentivizes affiliates to drive phone inquiries from potential customers who are interested in your courses.

- **Higher Intent Leads:** Phone inquiries often indicate a higher level of interest compared to website clicks or form submissions.

### Key Differences from Other Models:

- **Calls vs. Clicks or Conversions:** PPC focuses on phone calls, while standard PPC focuses on clicks, and PPS and PPL focus on conversions (sales or lead generation).

- **Marketing Strategies:** Affiliates promoting a PPC program might use tactics like telemarketing, social media marketing with call-to-action buttons, or content marketing that encourages phone inquiries.

**Additional Considerations:**

- **Cost-Effectiveness:** Ensure the commission you offer for calls is lower than your average profit margin to maintain profitability.
- **Call Tracking:** Implement a reliable call tracking system to attribute phone inquiries to specific affiliates and avoid paying for unqualified calls.
- **Clear Call Criteria:** Define what constitutes a "qualified lead" for phone inquiries to avoid disputes about commissions.

**Not Sale Price Based:**

- Unlike your description, commissions in affiliate marketing PPC are typically not based on a percentage of the sale price. They are usually a fixed dollar amount per qualified call.

**Sometimes Combined with Sales:**

- While the primary focus is on calls, some affiliate programs might offer an additional bonus commission if a call leads to a sale.

By understanding the unique aspects of Pay Per Call in affiliate marketing, you can decide if it's a suitable payout method for your online school.

Here are some additional tips:

- **Track Call Quality:** Monitor the quality and conversion rate of phone inquiries generated by affiliates.
- **Target Relevant Audiences:** Partner with affiliates who can reach potential customers who are a good fit for your online courses.
- **Provide Call Training:** Consider providing affiliates with training on how to effectively qualify leads over the phone.

Affiliate marketing can involve a variety of payout methods, and understanding them is crucial for building a successful program, especially for your online school. Here's a breakdown of Pay Per Impression (PPI) and some key points to consider:

**Pay Per Impression (PPI):**

- **Focus on Brand Awareness:** In affiliate marketing, PPI is not a common payout method. It's typically used in online advertising where advertisers pay publishers based on the number of times their ad is displayed on a website (impressions).
- **Limited Relevance in Affiliate Marketing:** For affiliate marketing, focusing on impressions doesn't directly incentivize affiliates to drive sales or qualified leads for your online courses.

### Alternative Payout Methods:

- **Pay Per Sale (PPS):** This is the most common method, where affiliates earn a commission only when a customer makes a purchase through their unique affiliate link.
- **Pay Per Click (PPC):** Affiliates earn a commission every time someone clicks on their affiliate link, regardless of whether they convert into a paying customer.
- **Pay Per Lead (PPL):** Affiliates get paid when a potential customer completes a desired action, such as filling out a lead generation form.

### Choosing the Right Method:

The best payout method for your online school depends on your goals and target audience. Here are some factors to consider:

- **Industry Standards:** Research what payout methods are typical for online courses in your niche.
- **Program Goals:** Align your payout method with your overall marketing goals (e.g., prioritize traffic generation, lead capture, or direct sales).
- **Affiliate Effort:** Consider the level of effort required for affiliates to promote your courses effectively.

### Focus on Conversions:

For your online school, PPS, PPC, or a hybrid model combining these might be more suitable as they directly incentivize actions that lead to sales or qualified leads.

### Additional Considerations:

- **Transparency:** Clearly communicate your commission rates and payout terms to your affiliates.
- **Timely Payouts:** Ensure affiliates receive their commissions promptly to maintain their satisfaction and motivation.
- **Affiliate Support:** Provide your affiliates with the resources and support they need to be successful, such as marketing materials, product training, and ongoing communication.

By understanding the different payout methods and focusing on models that incentivize sales or leads, you can create an effective affiliate marketing program for your online school.

Here are some additional tips:

- **Track Performance Data:** Monitor key metrics like sales volume, conversion rates, and affiliate performance. This data will help you determine the effectiveness of your program and make adjustments as needed.

- **Affiliate Feedback:** Seek feedback from your affiliates to understand their motivations and preferences. This can help you tailor your program to be more effective.
- **Regular Program Review:** Periodically review your affiliate program's overall structure, including commission rates, incentives, and marketing materials. Adapt and improve based on your findings and market conditions.

By implementing these strategies, you can leverage affiliate marketing effectively to reach a wider audience, generate leads, and achieve your online school's growth goals.

## THE BENEFITS

You're absolutely right. Affiliate marketing can be a powerful tool, but like any industry, it can attract unethical practices. Here's a breakdown of the ethical concerns and some strategies for qualifying your affiliate partners:

**Ethical Concerns in Affiliate Marketing:**

- **Misrepresentation:** Some affiliates might promote products or services with misleading claims or false promises, often associated with "get-rich-quick" schemes.
- **Low-Quality Products:** Affiliate marketing can be used to promote low-quality or ineffective products, which can damage your brand reputation if associated with them.
- **Spammy Tactics:** Unethical affiliates might resort to spammy marketing practices like unsolicited emails or misleading social media posts to promote products.

**Qualifying Your Affiliate Partners:**

- **Research and Due Diligence:** Before accepting affiliates, research their reputation, website content, and marketing practices. Ensure they align with your brand values and target audience.

- **Program Requirements:** Establish clear program guidelines that outline acceptable promotion practices and prohibit misleading claims or spam tactics.
- **Performance Monitoring:** Track the performance of your affiliates and monitor their marketing activities to identify any red flags.
- **Affiliate Reviews:** Utilize online resources and communities to check reviews and feedback about potential affiliates.
- **Direct Communication:** Maintain open communication with your affiliates and address any concerns about their marketing strategies.
Here are some additional tips:
- **Selective Approval Process:** Don't be afraid to be selective and have a clear approval process for new affiliates.
- **Performance-Based Commissions:** Consider structuring commissions based on performance metrics like sales or qualified leads. This discourages affiliates from relying on misleading tactics.
- **Affiliate Training:** Provide your affiliates with training on your products, brand messaging, and ethical marketing practices.
- **Termination Clause:** Include a termination clause in your affiliate agreements that allows you to remove affiliates who violate your program guidelines.
By implementing these strategies, you can build a network of ethical and trustworthy affiliates who will effectively promote your online school and protect your brand reputation.

Remember, a successful affiliate program relies on mutually beneficial partnerships. By carefully vetting your affiliates and promoting ethical marketing practices, you can create a program that benefits you, your affiliates, and ultimately your students.

## Affiliate marketing's popularity is surging, and for good reason. Here's a breakdown of the key points you mentioned and some additional thoughts:

### Performance-Based Advantage:
•**Cost-Effective Marketing:** Compared to traditional advertising, affiliate marketing offers a cost-effective way to reach a wider audience. You only pay affiliates when they generate sales or leads, minimizing upfront costs.
•**Motivated Sales Force:** Affiliates are incentivized to promote your courses effectively because their income depends on their performance. This creates a motivated sales force working to drive results for your online school.

- **Win-Win Partnership:** A well-structured affiliate program benefits both you and your affiliates. You gain access to a wider audience and increased sales, while affiliates earn commissions for promoting valuable products.

**Industry Statistics:**

- **Growing Popularity:** Market data confirms the rising popularity of affiliate marketing. As you mentioned, research shows a significant portion of advertisers consider it an integral part of their success.
- **Benefits for All:** Affiliate marketing offers advantages for businesses, affiliates, and consumers. Businesses gain wider reach, affiliates earn commissions, and consumers discover new products and services.

**Additional Considerations:**

- **Finding the Right Affiliates:** Building a successful affiliate network requires careful selection of partners who align with your brand and target audience.
- **Building Relationships:** Invest in fostering strong relationships with your affiliates. Provide them with the resources and support they need to be successful.
- **Tracking and Optimization:** Continuously monitor your affiliate program's performance and make adjustments as needed to optimize results.

By leveraging the performance-based nature of affiliate marketing and building strong partnerships with your affiliates, you can create a powerful marketing channel that drives growth for your online school. Here are some additional tips:

- **Offer Competitive Commissions:** Ensure your commission rates are attractive to incentivize high-quality affiliates to promote your courses.
- **Provide Marketing Materials:** Equip your affiliates with high-quality marketing materials such as banners, product descriptions, and social media content to make it easier for them to promote your courses.
- **Track Affiliate Traffic:** Utilize analytics tools to track the traffic and sales generated by your affiliates. This data will help you understand which affiliates are performing well and identify areas for improvement.

Remember, a successful affiliate marketing program is built on trust, transparency, and a shared focus on achieving results. By implementing effective strategies and fostering strong partnerships, you can leverage affiliate marketing to propel your online school forward.

You're absolutely right. The increasing popularity of affiliate marketing is a clear sign of its effectiveness. Let's delve into the different types of relationships between vendors (like you, the online course instructor) and affiliates to understand how they can benefit your online school:

**Types of Affiliate Relationships:**

- **One-Tier Model:** This is the most basic structure. You directly partner with individual affiliates who promote your courses.

- **Two-Tier Model:** In this model, you have both direct affiliates and "super affiliates" who recruit other affiliates to promote your courses and earn a commission on their sales as well.

- **Multi-Tier Model:** This extends the two-tier model by allowing for multiple levels of affiliate recruitment, creating a pyramid structure. However, this structure can become complex and is less common these days.

**Choosing the Right Model:**

The best model for your online school depends on your goals and resources. Here are some factors to consider:

- **Program Size:** If you're starting, a one-tier model might be sufficient. As your program grows, you can explore two-tier options.
- **Affiliate Management:** Two-tier and multi-tier models require more effort to manage and track affiliate performance.
- **Affiliate Network Marketing:** Consider joining an affiliate network that connects you with a large pool of potential affiliates. This can be a good option if you lack the resources to manage your own program.

**Benefits of Strong Affiliate Relationships:**

- **Increased Reach:** Affiliates can significantly expand your audience reach by leveraging their own established networks and marketing channels.
- **Targeted Marketing:** You can partner with affiliates who specialize in your niche, ensuring your courses are promoted to a highly relevant audience.
- **Improved Brand Awareness:** Affiliate marketing can effectively increase brand awareness for your online school and your courses.

**Building Strong Relationships:**

- **Clear Communication:** Maintain open communication with your affiliates and keep them informed about program updates, new courses, and promotional opportunities.
- **Supportive Resources:** Provide your affiliates with the resources they need to be successful, such as marketing materials, product training, and ongoing support.
- **Competitive Commissions:** Offer attractive commission rates to incentivize high-quality affiliates to promote your courses.

By understanding the different affiliate relationship models, fostering strong communication, and providing valuable support, you can create a win-win situation for your online school and your affiliate partners. This will ultimately lead to a more successful and sustainable affiliate marketing program for your online courses.

Here are some additional tips for exploring different affiliate relationships:

- **Research Other Programs:** See how other online course instructors structure their affiliate programs and learn from their successes.
- **Network with Affiliates:** Connect with potential affiliates in your niche and build relationships before formally inviting them to join your program.
- **Start Small and Scale Up:** Begin with a manageable affiliate network and gradually expand as you gain experience and resources.

Remember, a well-designed affiliate marketing program built on strong relationships can be a game-changer for your online school. It can help you reach a wider audience, establish brand recognition, and achieve your growth goals.

Here's a breakdown of the key points and some additional considerations:

**Unattached Affiliate Marketing:**

- **No Niche Expertise:** In this model, affiliates promote your online courses **without** necessarily having expertise or interest in your specific niche or subject matter.

- **Focus on Clicks:** Their primary motivation is typically earning commissions through pay-per-click (PPC) arrangements. They focus on driving clicks to your affiliate link, but may not actively promote or explain the value of your courses.

- **Limited Brand Alignment:** Since they lack niche expertise, their audience might not be a perfect fit for your courses, potentially leading to lower conversion rates.

- **Finding Unattached Affiliates:** Unattached affiliates are often found through advertising networks that connect publishers (website owners) with advertisers (like you).

**Considerations for Using Unattached Affiliates:**

- **Cost-Effectiveness:** Unattached affiliates can be a cost-effective way to generate website traffic, especially if the PPC commission rate is low.

- **Traffic Quality:** The quality of traffic driven by unattached affiliates can be unpredictable. Clicks might not translate into actual sales or qualified leads.

- **Limited Control:** You have less control over how your courses are presented by unattached affiliates, potentially leading to brand misrepresentation.

**Alternative Affiliate Types:**

- **Related Affiliate Marketing:** Affiliates have some connection to your niche but might not be recognized experts.

- **Involved Affiliate Marketing:** Affiliates are established authorities in your niche and actively promote and recommend your courses to their audience.

**Choosing the Right Affiliate Mix:**

You can consider a mix of affiliate types depending on your goals. Unattached affiliates might be suitable for initial brand awareness, while related or involved affiliates can drive targeted traffic and potentially higher conversions.

Here are some additional tips:

- **Track Affiliate Performance:** Monitor the traffic and sales generated by different affiliates to identify which ones are most effective.

- **Set Clear Guidelines:** Even with unattached affiliates, establish clear communication guidelines to ensure they present your courses accurately.

- **Prioritize Quality Over Quantity:** Focus on building relationships with high-quality affiliates who can drive valuable traffic, even if it means having a smaller network.

By understanding the pros and cons of unattached affiliate marketing and considering it as part of a broader affiliate strategy, you can create a more effective marketing program for your online school. Here's a breakdown of the key points and some additional considerations:

## Related Affiliate Marketing:

- **Niche Relevance:** In this model, affiliates have an online presence (blogs, websites, podcasts, social media) **related to your niche**, but they may not be established authorities or actively use your courses themselves.

- **Targeted Audience:** Their audience is likely interested in the same topics as your courses, creating a better fit than unattached affiliates.

- **Content Promotion:** Affiliates might promote your courses through various methods like banner ads, product reviews, or mentioning your courses in their content (even if they haven't personally used them).

- **Finding Related Affiliates:** You can find related affiliates by searching for blogs, websites, and social media influencers in your niche. Some affiliate networks can also help with this.

## Benefits of Related Affiliates:

- **Increased Relevance:** Their existing audience is more likely to be receptive to your courses compared to unattached affiliates.

- **Brand Affinity:** Since their niche aligns with yours, there's a better chance their audience trusts their recommendations.

- **Content Marketing Potential:** Related affiliates might create valuable content (reviews, comparisons) that promotes your courses organically.

## Considerations for Related Affiliates:

- **Expertise Level:** They might not have the deep expertise of involved affiliates, potentially impacting their ability to answer customer questions about your courses.

- **Promotion Strategies:** Monitor how they promote your courses and ensure they accurately represent your brand and course offerings.

## Related vs. Involved Affiliates:

- **Involved Affiliate Marketing:** Involved affiliates are established authorities in your niche who actively use and recommend your courses to their audience. They offer the highest level of trust and credibility.

## Choosing the Right Affiliate Mix:

The ideal affiliate mix depends on your goals. Consider using a combination of related affiliates for broader reach and potentially involved affiliates for targeted conversions.

**Here are some additional tips:**

- **Target High-Quality Affiliates:** Focus on partnering with related affiliates who have a good reputation and engaged audience in your niche.

- **Offer Incentives:** Consider offering additional incentives, such as bonuses or early access to new courses, to motivate related affiliates to promote your offerings more actively.

- **Provide Resources:** Equip related affiliates with the information and resources they need to effectively promote your courses, such as product demos, detailed descriptions, and marketing materials.

By understanding the value proposition of related affiliate marketing and integrating it into your strategy, you can expand your reach and attract potential students who are already interested in your niche.

You've absolutely nailed the concept of involved affiliate marketing! It's often considered the gold standard in affiliate partnerships for online courses. Here's a breakdown of the key points and some additional considerations:

**Involved Affiliate Marketing:**

- **Active Promotion by Experts:** Involved affiliates are established authorities in your niche who have **personally used and endorse your courses**. They actively promote them to their audience with genuine enthusiasm and credibility.

- **Highest Conversion Potential:** Since involved affiliates have deep knowledge of your courses and their benefits, they can effectively answer customer questions and drive higher conversion rates (sales or leads).

- **Increased Trust and Credibility:** Their personal experience with your courses fosters trust with their audience, leading to more effective promotions.

- **Finding Involved Affiliates:** You can identify involved affiliates by looking for positive reviews of your courses, active audience members in your online communities, or established figures in your niche who express interest in your offerings.

**Benefits of Involved Affiliates:**

- **Authentic Promotion:** Their genuine enthusiasm and expertise translate into more convincing and impactful promotions.

- **Targeted Audience Alignment:** Their audience is highly likely to be interested in your courses due to their niche expertise and trust in the affiliate.

- **Long-Term Partnerships:** Involved affiliates are often passionate about your niche and can become long-term partners who consistently promote your courses.

**Considerations for Involved Affiliates:**

- **Limited Availability:** Finding high-quality involved affiliates can be challenging due to their established niche presence.
- **Commission Structure:** Consider offering competitive commission rates or additional incentives to attract and motivate involved affiliates.

**Building Strong Relationships:**

- **Open Communication:** Maintain regular communication with involved affiliates and keep them updated on new courses, promotions, and marketing materials.
- **Support and Recognition:** Provide them with the resources and support they need to be successful. Publicly recognize their contributions to your program.

**Complementary Affiliate Mix:**

A well-rounded affiliate program might include a mix of involved affiliates for targeted conversions, related affiliates for broader reach, and potentially unattached affiliates for cost-effective brand awareness (especially if the PPC commission rate is low).

**Here are some additional tips:**

- **Offer Early Access:** Consider providing involved affiliates with early access to new courses so they can create in-depth reviews and promotions.
- **Content Collaboration:** Explore co-creating valuable content (webinars, blog posts) with involved affiliates to leverage their expertise and reach a wider audience.
- **Community Building:** Foster a sense of community among your affiliates, including involved affiliates. This can encourage collaboration and knowledge sharing.

By actively seeking out and building strong relationships with involved affiliates, you can create a powerful marketing force for your online school. Their genuine enthusiasm and expertise will translate into increased sales and brand loyalty for your online courses.

## Involved affiliate marketing is indeed the ideal scenario for online course creators seeking long-term success through affiliate partnerships. Here's a summary of the key points and some additional thoughts:

### Full-On Engagement Through Involved Affiliates:

•**Benefits for All:** Involved affiliates are passionate about your niche, have used your courses, and genuinely believe in their value. This translates into authentic promotions, increased trust with their audience, and ultimately, higher conversion rates for your online school.

- **Building Relationships:** The key to success lies in fostering strong relationships with involved affiliates. Provide them with support, resources, and recognition to keep them motivated and engaged in promoting your courses.
- **Long-Term Growth:** Involved affiliates can become your biggest brand advocates, driving consistent sales and contributing to the long-term growth of your online school.

**Why Involved Affiliates Win:**

- **Credibility and Trust:** Their personal experience with your courses builds trust with their audience, making their promotions more effective.
- **Targeted Audience:** Their established niche expertise ensures their audience is highly likely to be interested in your offerings.
- **Unconsciously Attractive:** By genuinely promoting courses they believe in, involved affiliates naturally make them more attractive to potential students.

**Building a Network of Involved Affiliates:**

- **Identify Potential Partners:** Look for positive reviews of your courses, active audience members in your online communities, or established figures in your niche who express interest.
- **Offer Competitive Incentives:** Consider attractive commission rates or additional incentives to attract and motivate high-quality involved affiliates.
- **Open Communication and Support:** Maintain regular communication, keep them updated, and provide them with the resources and support they need to be successful.

**Complementary Affiliate Mix:**

While involved affiliates are ideal, a well-rounded program might also include:

- **Related Affiliates:** For broader reach within your niche.
- **Unattached Affiliates:** For cost-effective brand awareness (use cautiously and with clear communication guidelines).

**The Road to Success:**

By prioritizing involved affiliate marketing, building strong relationships, and creating a supportive environment, you can develop a powerful network of advocates who will propel your online school forward. Remember, a win-win partnership with your affiliates is key to achieving sustainable growth and success.

Here are some additional tips for building a successful network of involved affiliates:

- **Offer Exclusive Content:** Provide involved affiliates with exclusive content (like bonuses or early access to new courses) that they can use to create even more compelling promotions.
- **Track Performance and Reward Results:** Monitor the performance of your affiliates and offer additional rewards or recognition for those who consistently drive high-quality sales or leads.
- **Create a Community:** Foster a sense of community among your affiliates where they can connect, collaborate, and share best practices.

By implementing these strategies and focusing on building genuine relationships with involved affiliates, you can transform your affiliate marketing program into a powerful engine for growth for your online school.

You're absolutely right! Affiliate marketing offers a cost-effective and performance-based approach to marketing, making it a safe and attractive option for many businesses, especially online schools. Here's a breakdown of the key points and some additional considerations:

**Cost-Effectiveness and Reduced Risk:**

- **Pay for Performance:** A core advantage of affiliate marketing is that you only pay affiliates when they generate a sale or qualified lead. This minimizes upfront costs and financial risk compared to traditional marketing methods like advertising where you pay regardless of results.

- **Scalability:** You can easily scale your affiliate program up or down based on your budget. As your business grows, you can increase commission rates or expand your affiliate network.

- **Comparison to Traditional Marketing:** Affiliate marketing is often significantly cheaper than traditional marketing methods like TV ads, radio commercials, or print advertising, which typically require substantial upfront investments.

**Additional Considerations:**

- **Affiliate Management:** Managing affiliate relationships, tracking performance, and providing support requires time and effort.
- **Finding Quality Affiliates:** Building a network of high-quality affiliates who effectively promote your courses is crucial for success.
- **Performance Optimization:** Continuously monitor and optimize your affiliate program to ensure you're attracting the right affiliates and maximizing your return on investment (ROI).

**Overall, affiliate marketing offers a safe and cost-effective way to reach a wider audience and generate sales or leads for your online school.** Here are some additional tips to keep in mind:

- **Set Clear Expectations:** Establish clear program guidelines that outline commission rates, tracking methods, and prohibited marketing practices.
- **Provide Marketing Materials:** Equip your affiliates with high-quality marketing materials like banners, product descriptions, and social media content to make it easier for them to promote your courses.
- **Track and Analyze Performance:** Use data and analytics to track the performance of your affiliate program and identify areas for improvement.

By implementing these strategies and focusing on building a strong foundation, you can leverage the cost-effective advantages of affiliate marketing to propel your online school forward.

# Affiliate marketing is a fantastic example of a win-win scenario.

# Here's a breakdown of the key points and some additional thoughts:

**Win-Win Partnership:**

•**Vendor Benefits:** As you mentioned, vendors (like you, the online course instructor) gain access to a wider audience, increased sales or leads, and cost-effective marketing compared to traditional methods.

•**Affiliate Benefits:** Affiliates earn commissions for promoting your courses, and they only invest their time and effort if they generate successful referrals.

•**Mutually Beneficial Agreement:** A well-structured affiliate agreement outlines expectations, commission rates, and terms that benefit both parties.

**Additional Considerations:**

•**Building Trust and Transparency:** Maintaining open communication, transparency, and trust with your affiliates is key to a successful long-term partnership.

•**Affiliate Satisfaction:** Providing ongoing support, resources, and opportunities for your affiliates to succeed leads to higher affiliate satisfaction and program effectiveness.

**Beyond the Win-Win:**

- **Value for Customers:** Ultimately, a successful affiliate marketing program benefits the customer as well. Affiliates are incentivized to promote high-quality courses that solve customer problems or fulfill their needs.

**Here are some additional tips for fostering a win-win partnership:**

- **Offer Competitive Commissions:** Ensure your commission rates are attractive to incentivize high-quality affiliates to promote your courses.
- **Provide Excellent Customer Support:** Invest in excellent customer support so that leads generated by affiliates have a positive experience with your courses.
- **Recognize Top Performers:** Publicly acknowledge and reward your top-performing affiliates to show your appreciation and motivate them to continue their efforts.

By focusing on building a win-win partnership with your affiliates and prioritizing customer satisfaction, you can create a sustainable and successful affiliate marketing program that benefits everyone involved.

Affiliate marketing is a powerful tool for expanding your target audience. Here's a breakdown of the key points you mentioned and some additional thoughts:

- **Reaching New Audiences:** By partnering with affiliates who have established networks in your niche, you can gain access to a much larger pool of potential customers than you could reach on your own.

- **Niche Expertise:** Affiliates are often niche experts with dedicated audiences who trust their recommendations. This can lead to higher conversion rates (sales or leads) compared to marketing to a broader audience.

- **Increased Brand Awareness:** Affiliate marketing can significantly increase brand awareness for your online school and your courses. As affiliates promote your offerings across their channels, your brand name gets seen by a wider audience.

**Thinking Beyond Numbers:**

- **Quality over Quantity:** It's important to focus on finding the right affiliates who align with your brand and target audience, rather than simply the ones with the biggest networks.

- **Building Relationships:** Strong relationships with your affiliates are key to a successful program. Provide them with the resources and support they need to effectively promote your courses.

**Here are some additional tips for expanding your target audience through affiliate marketing:**

- **Target High-Quality Affiliates:** Focus on partnering with affiliates who have a good reputation and engaged audience in your niche.

- **Offer Targeted Marketing Materials:** Provide affiliates with marketing materials that are tailored to their specific audience segments.

- **Track and Analyze Performance:** Monitor which affiliates are driving the most qualified traffic and conversions, and adjust your strategies accordingly.

By implementing these strategies, you can leverage affiliate marketing to effectively expand your target audience, reach new potential students, and achieve your growth goals for your online school.

Affiliate marketing can be a powerful tool for online course creators to achieve greater professional independence. Here's a breakdown of the key points and some additional considerations:

**Professional Independence:**

- **Reduced Reliance on Direct Sales:** By utilizing affiliate marketing, you can diversify your marketing channels and reduce dependence on selling courses solely through your online school or personal marketing efforts.

- **Expanded Reach and Brand Awareness:** Affiliate networks can significantly increase your reach and brand awareness within your niche, potentially propelling you to higher tiers of the online market.

- **Multiple Revenue Streams:** Affiliate marketing creates an additional revenue stream for your online school, making you less reliant on individual course sales or promotions.

**Considerations for Professional Independence:**

- **Building a Strong Affiliate Network:** Developing a network of high-performing affiliates requires time, effort, and strategic selection.

- **Maintaining Brand Control:** While affiliates promote your courses, ensure they accurately represent your brand and course offerings.

- **Focus on Quality over Quantity:** Prioritize building relationships with quality affiliates who align with your brand rather than just focusing on large networks.

**Additional Strategies for Professional Independence:**

- **Develop High-Quality Courses:** Creating valuable and effective courses is the foundation for success in affiliate marketing. Satisfied affiliates are more likely to enthusiastically promote your offerings.

- **Invest in Customer Support:** Provide excellent customer support to ensure a positive experience for students referred by your affiliates. This will strengthen your brand reputation and encourage repeat business.

- **Continuously Improve:** Regularly monitor your affiliate program's performance, analyze data, and make adjustments to optimize results.

By implementing these strategies, you can leverage affiliate marketing to achieve greater professional independence, expand your reach, and establish your online school as a respected player in your niche. Remember, building a successful affiliate program requires dedication and ongoing effort, but the potential rewards for professional independence and market growth can be significant.

## There can be some indirect benefits to SEO, but it's important to clarify some aspects:

**Affiliate Marketing and SEO: An Indirect Impact**

**•Increased Brand Awareness:** Affiliate marketing can significantly increase brand awareness for your online school. As affiliates promote your courses across various channels, your brand name is seen more often, which can potentially improve search rankings over time due to increased brand recognition.

**•Potential for Backlinks:** In some cases, affiliates might create content (blog posts, reviews) that link back to your website. These backlinks can be a positive SEO factor, but it's not guaranteed and shouldn't be the primary focus.

**•Focus on Quality Content:** For long-term SEO success, prioritize creating high-quality, informative content on your website that educates potential students and establishes you as an authority in your niche.

### Limited Direct Impact on Search Rankings

**•Affiliate Link Sharing:** Simply sharing affiliate links doesn't directly influence search rankings. Search engines focus on the content and quality of your website.

**•Unethical Practices:** Avoid practices like keyword stuffing or link buying through affiliates, as these can harm your SEO in the long run.

### Here are some additional tips for SEO success:

**•Keyword Research:** Identify relevant keywords that potential students are searching for and optimize your website content accordingly.

**•Content Marketing Strategy:** Develop a content marketing strategy that creates valuable content (blog posts, videos) that educates your target audience and positions you as an expert.

**•Technical SEO:** Ensure your website has a clean and mobile-friendly design, with proper technical SEO practices implemented.

### Building a Sustainable Strategy:

By focusing on creating high-quality content, building a strong brand reputation, and implementing proper SEO practices, you can create a sustainable marketing strategy that drives organic traffic and student acquisition for your online school, alongside the benefits of affiliate marketing

## Affiliate marketing offers a relatively easy entry point for online course creators, especially compared to some other marketing methods. Here's a breakdown of the key points and some additional considerations:

### Accessibility for Newcomers:

**•Low Barrier to Entry:** Compared to other marketing strategies, affiliate marketing has a lower barrier to entry. The core concepts are relatively easy to understand.

**•Learning Curve:** While the fundamentals are accessible, mastering affiliate marketing does involve some learning and experimentation. It's important to track your results, analyze data, and continuously refine your approach.

**•No Pre-Launch Following Required:** Affiliate marketing allows you to tap into established audiences of your affiliates, even if you don't have a large pre-launch following yourself.

### Considerations and Additional Tips:

**•Finding Quality Affiliates:** The success of your program hinges on finding high-quality affiliates who align with your brand and niche. Take time to identify the right partners.

**•Building Relationships:** Invest in fostering strong relationships with your affiliates. Provide them with the resources and support they need to succeed in promoting your courses.

**•Performance Tracking and Optimization:** Continuously monitor the performance of your affiliate program. Analyze data to identify areas for improvement and optimize your strategies for better results.

### Additional Strategies for Success:

•**Develop High-Quality Courses:** Creating valuable and effective courses is the foundation for success in affiliate marketing. Satisfied affiliates are more likely to enthusiastically promote your offerings.

•**Offer Competitive Commissions:** Ensure your commission rates are attractive to incentivize high-quality affiliates to promote your courses.

•**Provide Marketing Materials:** Equip your affiliates with high-quality marketing materials such as banners, product descriptions, and social media content to make it easier for them to promote your courses.

By focusing on building strong relationships, offering valuable resources, and continuously optimizing your program, you can leverage the ease of entry that affiliate marketing offers and turn it into a powerful marketing tool for your online school. Remember, even though the core concepts are easy to grasp, mastering affiliate marketing takes dedication and ongoing effort. However, the potential rewards for your online school's growth can be significant.

Affiliate marketing is a fantastic tool for increasing brand visibility and achieving significant growth for your online school. Here's a breakdown of the key points and some additional thoughts:

## Growth Hacking with Affiliate Marketing:

- **Rapid Brand Exposure:** Partnering with affiliates allows you to tap into their established networks and reach a wider audience quickly. This can significantly increase brand awareness and visibility for your online school.

- **Industry Recognition:** As your brand is promoted by reputable affiliates within your niche, it can lead to increased recognition and establish you as a respected player in the industry.

- **Growth Hacking Potential:** Affiliate marketing leverages the power of other people's networks, making it a cost-effective way to achieve significant growth compared to traditional marketing methods.

## Additional Considerations:

- **Quality over Quantity:** Focus on building relationships with high-quality affiliates who have a good reputation and engaged audience in your niche, rather than simply the ones with the largest networks.

- **Brand Alignment:** Ensure your affiliates accurately represent your brand values and course offerings to maintain brand consistency.

## Strategies for Increased Brand Visibility:

- **Targeted Affiliate Selection:** Carefully select affiliates whose audience aligns with your ideal student profile. This ensures your brand is seen by the right people.

- **Incentivize Social Media Promotion:** Encourage affiliates to promote your courses on social media platforms to maximize brand visibility.

- **Co-Branded Marketing Initiatives:** Explore co-branded marketing initiatives with your affiliates, such as webinars or social media campaigns, to further amplify brand exposure.

## Building a Sustainable Brand:

By focusing on building strong relationships with your affiliates, selecting the right partners, and implementing strategic marketing initiatives, you can leverage affiliate marketing to significantly increase brand visibility for your online school. Remember, building a strong brand takes time and consistent effort, but affiliate marketing can be a powerful growth accelerator in your journey. Here are some additional tips:

- **Create High-Quality Content:** Develop valuable and informative content (blog posts, videos) that showcases your expertise and establishes you as a thought leader in your niche. This strengthens your brand reputation and attracts potential students.

- **Invest in Customer Experience:** Provide a positive customer experience for students referred by your affiliates. Satisfied students are more likely to recommend your courses to others, organically enhancing your brand image.

By implementing these strategies, you can use affiliate marketing to not only increase brand visibility but also build a strong and lasting brand reputation for your online school.

Affiliate marketing allows you to tap into a vast network of promoters, creating a powerful force for your online school that goes beyond traditional advertising methods. Here's a breakdown of the key points and some additional considerations:

**Beyond Traditional Advertising:**

- **Amplified Reach:** Affiliate marketing lets you leverage the reach and audience of numerous affiliates, significantly expanding your promotional reach compared to relying solely on your own advertising efforts.

- **Scalability:** Your affiliate network can grow alongside your business. As you add new affiliates, you can exponentially increase your brand exposure.

- **Diverse Audiences:** Affiliates often cater to specific audience segments within your niche. This allows you to target a wider range of potential students with personalized messaging.

**Considerations and Additional Tips:**

- **Affiliate Selection:** Carefully select affiliates who align with your brand and target audience to ensure effective promotion.

- **Affiliate Management:** Building and maintaining relationships with your affiliates is crucial for program success. Provide them with resources, support, and motivation.

**The Power of 50 Affiliates:**

- **Imagine the scenario you described:** 50 affiliates promoting your courses on their websites simultaneously. This creates a massive wave of brand exposure and can lead to a significant increase in traffic and potential sales.

**Additional Strategies for Success:**

- **Develop Targeted Marketing Materials:** Provide affiliates with a variety of marketing materials tailored to different audience segments.

- **Offer Ongoing Training and Support:** Invest in ongoing training and support for your affiliates. Equip them with the knowledge and skills they need to effectively promote your courses.
- **Create a Thriving Affiliate Community:** Foster a sense of community among your affiliates. This can encourage collaboration, knowledge sharing, and overall program success.

### Building a Powerful Network:

By focusing on quality over quantity, nurturing affiliate relationships, and providing ongoing support, you can transform your affiliate network into a powerful marketing engine that drives consistent growth for your online school.

Here are some additional tips for building a strong affiliate network:

- **Offer Competitive Commission Rates:** Ensure your commission rates are attractive to incentivize high-quality affiliates to promote your courses.
- **Recognize Top Performers:** Publicly acknowledge and reward your top-performing affiliates to show your appreciation and motivate them to continue their efforts.
- **Track and Analyze Performance:** Monitor the performance of your affiliates and identify areas for improvement. This allows you to optimize your program and maximize your return on investment (ROI). By implementing these strategies, you can leverage the power of affiliate marketing to move beyond traditional advertising and create a network of dedicated promoters who can significantly amplify your brand's reach and propel your online school forward.

# AFFILIATE PROGRAM

Setting a commission structure is a crucial aspect of affiliate marketing and a topic with a lot of discussion. Here's a breakdown of the key points you mentioned and some additional thoughts:

### The Importance of Commission Structure:

- **Financial Incentive:** Commission rates are the primary motivator for affiliates. An attractive commission structure is crucial for attracting and retaining high-quality affiliates who will actively promote your courses.
- **Profitability for You:** While you want to incentivize affiliates, you also need to ensure your commission

rates are sustainable for your business model.

- **Finding the Right Balance:** The ideal commission structure balances your needs with those of your affiliates, creating a win-win scenario.

### Considerations for Setting Commission Rates:

- **Industry Standards:** Research commission rates offered by similar online course creators in your niche. This provides a benchmark for setting your own rates.
- **Course Value:** Consider the cost of your courses when determining commission rates. Higher-priced courses may warrant higher commission percentages.
- **Affiliate Performance:** Explore tiered commission structures that reward high-performing affiliates with increased commission rates.

### Beyond a Flat Rate:

- **Flexibility and Negotiation:** A one-size-fits-all approach to commission rates might not be ideal. Be open to negotiating with high-performing affiliates or those with established audiences.
- **Performance-Based Incentives:** Consider offering additional incentives, such as bonuses for exceeding sales targets, to further motivate affiliates.

### Moving Beyond Commission Rates:

- **Additional Benefits:** Supplement attractive commission rates with additional benefits like early access to new courses, free marketing materials, or exclusive discounts.
- **Building Relationships:** Invest in building strong relationships with your affiliates. Open communication, ongoing support, and recognition go a long way in creating a successful affiliate program.

### Remember:

Setting a competitive and well-structured commission plan is just one piece of the puzzle. By fostering strong partnerships and offering ongoing value to your affiliates, you can create a program that benefits everyone involved.

Here are some additional tips for establishing your commission structure:

- **Track Performance:** Monitor the performance of your affiliate program and adjust commission rates as needed to optimize results.
- **Conduct A/B Testing:** Test different commission structures to see what motivates your affiliates the most.
- **Seek Expert Advice:** Consider consulting with affiliate marketing experts for guidance on setting commission rates and building a successful program.

By implementing these strategies, you can move beyond simply setting a commission structure and create a comprehensive affiliate marketing program that attracts high-quality partners, drives sales, and propels your online school forward.

You're absolutely right! Competitor research is a crucial step in setting your affiliate marketing commission structure. Here's a breakdown of the key points and some additional considerations:

### Learning from the Competition:

- **Benchmarking:** Researching your competitors' commission rates provides a valuable benchmark for setting your own rates. You'll get a sense of what's considered standard within your niche.
- **Understanding Strategies:** By analyzing competitor programs, you can understand their strategies and identify potential areas for differentiation.
- **Market Insights:** Competitor research can offer insights into current market trends and affiliate expectations regarding commission structures.

### Beyond Just Rates:

- **Look Beyond Numbers:** While commission rates are important, don't solely focus on copying competitor numbers. Consider the overall structure, including incentives, payment terms, and affiliate support offered.
- **Identify Strengths and Weaknesses:** Analyze your competitors' strengths and weaknesses in their affiliate programs. This can help you develop a program that stands out.

### Using Insights for Advantage:

- **Competitive Advantage:** Once you understand the competitive landscape, you can position your program strategically. Offer a more attractive commission structure, additional benefits, or superior affiliate support.
- **Targeted Research:** Focus your research on competitors who target a similar audience or offer courses comparable to yours. Their approach will be most relevant.

### Additional Strategies:

- **Direct Outreach:** Consider reaching out to successful affiliates in your niche (not necessarily promoting your competitors) to gather insights on commission structures and program preferences.
- **Industry Reports:** Look for industry reports or surveys that analyze affiliate marketing trends and commission rates in your niche.

### Remember:

The goal of competitor research isn't to copy blindly, but to gain valuable insights that help you develop a strong and competitive affiliate marketing program for your online school.

Here are some additional tips for conducting effective competitor research:

- **Focus on Reputable Sources:** Rely on credible sources like industry publications, marketing blogs, or affiliate marketing forums for accurate competitor data.

- **Go Beyond Numbers:** Use competitor research tools to analyze competitor websites, marketing materials, and social media presence to understand their overall affiliate marketing strategy.
- **Track Changes Over Time:** Monitor your competitors' programs over time to identify any changes they make to their commission structures or affiliate offerings.

By implementing these strategies, you can leverage competitor research to set a competitive commission structure, develop a differentiated program, and attract high-quality affiliates to your online school's affiliate marketing program.

Here's a breakdown of the key points:

### The EPC Equation:

- **Factors Influencing EPC:** EPC is not just about the commission rate you offer affiliates. It's also significantly impacted by your website's conversion rate (visitors who turn into sales or leads).
- **Conversion Rate Matters:** A higher conversion rate means more visitors to your website are converted into paying customers, even with a lower commission rate. This can lead to a higher EPC.
- **Optimizing for Conversions:** Focus on optimizing your website and landing pages to improve conversion rates. This will maximize the return on investment (ROI) for your affiliate marketing program, regardless of the specific commission rate you offer.

### Additional Considerations:

- **Cost per Acquisition (CPA):** Consider your customer acquisition cost (CPA) when setting commission rates. Ensure your commission rates allow you to acquire new students profitably.
- **Affiliate Traffic Quality:** The quality of traffic driven by your affiliates also impacts EPC. High-quality, targeted traffic is more likely to convert, even at a lower commission rate.

### Strategies for Improving EPC:

- **A/B Testing:** Test different landing page elements, calls to action, and website layouts to identify what converts best.
- **Targeted Content:** Create targeted content that resonates with your ideal student profile to attract high-quality traffic.
- **Offer Value:** Provide valuable content and resources on your website to build trust and encourage conversions.

### Remember:

A successful affiliate marketing program requires a holistic approach. While commission rates are important, optimizing your website for conversions and attracting high-quality traffic are equally crucial for maximizing your EPC and achieving your program's goals.

Here are some additional tips for improving your EPC:

- **Track and Analyze Data:** Continuously monitor your affiliate program's performance and analyze data to identify areas for improvement.
- **Provide Affiliate Support:** Equip your affiliates with the tools and resources they need to drive high-quality traffic to your website.
- **Offer Performance Incentives:** Consider offering additional incentives to affiliates who drive high-converting traffic or generate sales from qualified leads.

By focusing on these aspects, you can create a well-rounded affiliate marketing program that optimizes EPC, attracts valuable affiliates, and drives sustainable growth for your online school.

# A well-designed commission structure should align with your online school's key objectives and incentivize the behaviors that drive your success. Here's a breakdown of the concept of tiered commissions and some additional considerations:

**Tiered Commission Structures:**

- **Rewarding Performance:** Tiered commissions structures reward affiliates based on their performance. High performers (e.g., those who generate high sales or qualified leads) receive higher commission rates.
- **Aligning with Objectives:** You can design tiers based on various objectives, such as sales volume, student quality, or promotion of specific courses.
- **Motivating Affiliates:** Tiered structures motivate affiliates to strive for better performance to unlock higher commission rates.

**Examples of Tiered Structures:**

- **Sales Volume Tiers:** Offer increasing commission rates based on the number of sales generated by an affiliate.
- **Lead Quality Tiers:** Reward affiliates who generate qualified leads that convert into paying students with higher commissions.
- **Course-Specific Tiers:** Offer higher commission rates for promoting your high-value or in-demand courses.

**Additional Considerations:**

- **Transparency:** Clearly communicate your tiered commission structure to all affiliates to ensure understanding and fairness.
- **Earning Potential:** Ensure each tier offers a realistic and achievable earning potential to motivate affiliates.
- **Track and Analyze Performance:** Monitor affiliate performance data to evaluate the effectiveness of your tiered structure and make adjustments as needed.

**Beyond Tiers:**

- **Bonus Incentives:** Consider offering additional bonuses on top of tiered commissions for exceeding targets or achieving specific goals.
- **Long-Term Relationships:** Develop long-term relationships with your top-performing affiliates through ongoing support and recognition.

**Remember:**

A well-designed commission structure is a powerful tool for attracting high-quality affiliates and achieving your online school's growth objectives. By aligning your structure with your key goals and offering a clear path to higher earnings, you can create a program that motivates affiliates, drives results, and helps your online school thrive.

Here are some additional tips for crafting your commission structure:

- **Start with Industry Benchmarks:** Research commission rates in your niche to establish a baseline for your structure.
- **Consider Long-Term Sustainability:** Ensure your commission rates are profitable for your business model in the long run.
- **Seek Expert Advice:** Consider consulting with affiliate marketing experts for guidance on designing a commission structure that aligns with your specific goals.

By implementing these strategies, you can create a commission structure that reflects your key objectives, attracts high-performing affiliates, and fuels the growth of your online school.

You're absolutely right! Communication and building relationships are crucial aspects of successful affiliate marketing. Here's a breakdown of the importance of talking to your affiliates and some additional considerations:

## Open Communication with Affiliates:

- **One-on-One Interaction:** Regularly communicating with your affiliates on an individual basis fosters stronger relationships, builds trust, and allows you to understand their needs and challenges.

- **Negotiation Opportunities:** Open communication allows for mutually beneficial negotiation on commission rates, promotional strategies, or other program aspects.

- **Identifying Top Performers:** Through communication, you can identify affiliates who are making a significant impact and personalize your approach to maximize their contribution.

## Strategies for Effective Communication:

- **Regular Check-Ins:** Schedule regular calls or video conferences with your affiliates to discuss performance, answer questions, and offer support.

- **Personalized Communication:** Avoid a "one-size-fits-all" approach. Tailor your communication to address each affiliate's specific needs and concerns.

- **Openness to Feedback:** Encourage your affiliates to provide feedback on your program and be receptive to suggestions for improvement.

## Working Closely with Top Performers:

- **Targeted Strategies:** Develop specific goals and strategies in collaboration with your top-performing affiliates to further maximize their results.

- **Incentive Programs:** Consider offering additional incentives, such as bonuses or exclusive benefits, to top performers to maintain their motivation and engagement.

- **Knowledge Sharing:** Facilitate knowledge sharing among your affiliates, allowing top performers to mentor or share insights with others.

## Building a Thriving Community:

- **Affiliate Forums:** Create an online forum or community space for affiliates to connect, share ideas, and support each other.
- **Industry Events:** Consider inviting your top-performing affiliates to industry events or conferences to further strengthen relationships and provide valuable learning opportunities.
- **Recognition Programs:** Publicly acknowledge and reward your top-performing affiliates to show appreciation and motivate others.

### Remember:

Your affiliates are valuable partners in your online school's success. By investing in open communication, building strong relationships, and offering ongoing support, you can create a thriving affiliate program that drives results and benefits everyone involved.

Here are some additional tips for communicating effectively with your affiliates:

- **Provide Clear Communication:** Ensure your communication with affiliates is clear, concise, and professional.
- **Be Responsive:** Respond promptly to affiliate inquiries and questions to demonstrate your commitment to their success.
- **Offer Valuable Resources:** Provide affiliates with access to marketing materials, training resources, and other tools they need to promote your courses effectively.

By implementing these strategies, you can move beyond basic communication and build a collaborative and supportive environment that empowers your affiliates to achieve peak performance and propel your online school forward.

A successful affiliate program requires a dynamic approach to commission structures. Here's a breakdown of the concept of temporary commission increases and some additional considerations:

### Strategic Commission Adjustments:

- **Flexibility Matters:** Commission rates shouldn't be static. Strategic adjustments can incentivize affiliates and achieve specific program goals.
- **Temporary Increases:** Offering temporary commission increases for new course launches or sales pushes can motivate affiliates to promote these offerings more heavily.
- **Sales Incentives:** Consider offering additional sales incentives, like bonuses or tiered payouts, to create a window of opportunity and drive sales quickly.

### Balancing Interests:

- **Profitability:** Ensure any temporary increases or sales incentives remain within a profitable range for your business model.
- **Sustainability:** Don't rely solely on temporary boosts. Develop a sustainable commission structure that incentivizes ongoing promotion.

### Additional Strategies for New Course Launches:

- **Early Access:** Offer your top affiliates early access to new courses so they can create high-quality promotional content.
- **Dedicated Resources:** Provide affiliates with dedicated marketing materials and resources specifically tailored for promoting your new course.
- **Training Webinars:** Host training webinars for affiliates to familiarize them with your new course content and key selling points.

### Moving Beyond Temporary Incentives:

- **Long-Term Value:** While temporary incentives can be effective, focus on building long-term value for your affiliates through ongoing support, relationship building, and a strong commission structure.
- **Performance-Based Rewards:** Consider incorporating performance-based rewards into your regular commission structure to incentivize ongoing sales efforts.

### Remember:

A well-designed commission structure is a powerful tool, but it's just one piece of the puzzle. By offering ongoing value, building strong relationships, and strategically using temporary incentives, you can create a dynamic and successful affiliate program that drives sales of your new courses and fuels the growth of your online school.

Here are some additional tips for using temporary commission increases effectively:

- **Clear Communication:** Clearly communicate the terms and duration of any temporary commission increases or sales incentives to your affiliates.
- **Track Results:** Monitor the impact of temporary commission increases on sales and affiliate performance.
- **Data-Driven Decisions:** Use data to determine the effectiveness of temporary incentives and adjust your strategies accordingly.

By implementing these strategies, you can use temporary commission increases strategically to achieve specific goals, while still maintaining a sustainable and rewarding affiliate program for your online school.

You're absolutely right! Payment periods are a crucial aspect of affiliate marketing programs, impacting both you and your affiliates. Here's a breakdown of the concept and some additional considerations:

### Strategic Payment Periods:

- **Refund Buffer:** Setting a payment period with a buffer (e.g., 30 days) allows you to account for potential refunds or chargebacks before paying commissions.
- **Cash Flow Management:** Payment periods can be used to manage your cash flow. A longer period gives you time to collect revenue before paying out commissions.
- **Motivational Factor:** Faster payouts can incentivize affiliates, especially for those who rely on regular income from their promotional efforts.

### Finding the Right Balance:

- **Industry Standards:** Research common payment periods in your niche to establish a baseline.
- **Affiliate Expectations:** Consider your affiliates' needs and preferences when determining an appropriate payment period.
- **Transparency:** Clearly outline the payment period in your affiliate agreement to avoid confusion.

### Additional Considerations:

- **Payment Methods:** Offer a variety of payment methods (e.g., PayPal, bank transfer) to cater to your affiliates' preferences.
- **Timely Payments:** Even with a buffer period, strive to process affiliate payments promptly once the buffer window has passed.
- **Net Payment Terms:** Consider using "net" payment terms (e.g., Net 30), which means affiliates are paid within a specific timeframe (e.g., 30 days) after the end of the month in which commissions were earned.

### Optimizing Your Program:

- **Track Performance:** Monitor the impact of your payment period on affiliate performance and program success.
- **Gather Feedback:** Seek feedback from your affiliates on their preferences regarding payment timing.
- **Be Flexible:** Within reason, consider adjusting your payment period based on data and affiliate feedback to optimize your program.

### Remember:

The ideal payment period balances your cash flow needs with the motivational benefits of faster payouts for your affiliates. By being transparent, offering flexibility, and processing payments promptly, you can establish trust and encourage strong participation in your affiliate program.

Here are some additional tips for managing affiliate payment periods:

- **Automate Payments:** If possible, automate affiliate payouts to ensure timely and efficient processing.

- **Communicate Clearly:** Clearly communicate any changes to the payment period to your affiliates well in advance.
- **Track Payment History:** Maintain accurate records of affiliate payments made to ensure transparency and avoid disputes.

By implementing these strategies, you can leverage payment periods to your benefit, maintain a healthy cash flow, and create a program that incentivizes your affiliates and drives growth for your online school.

You've raised a valid concern about the potential downsides of a 30-day payment buffer for affiliate programs, particularly the risk of chargebacks. Here's a breakdown of the issue and some alternative approaches to consider:

## The Chargeback Challenge:

- **Refund Buffer:** A 30-day buffer allows you to process refunds or chargebacks before paying out commissions. This protects your business.
- **Affiliate Impact:** Longer payment periods can negatively impact affiliates who rely on regular income.

## Alternative Payment Schedules:

- **Faster Payouts:** Consider a shorter payment buffer (e.g., 14 days) to incentivize affiliates while mitigating some chargeback risk.
- **Recurring Commissions:** For subscriptions or membership products, explore recurring commission payouts based on active subscriptions.
- **Hybrid Model:** Consider a hybrid model with a shorter initial payout window (e.g., 14 days) followed by a final reconciliation after the full refund buffer period (e.g., 30 days).

## Mitigating Chargeback Risk:

- **Clear Refund Policy:** Clearly outline your refund policy in your affiliate agreement and on your website to manage customer expectations.
- **High-Quality Affiliates:** Focus on recruiting and partnering with high-quality affiliates who promote your courses ethically.
- **Customer Satisfaction:** Prioritize customer satisfaction by delivering high-quality courses and excellent customer support to minimize chargebacks.

## Finding the Right Balance:

- **Evaluate Options:** Weigh the benefits of faster payouts for affiliates against the risk of chargebacks to determine the optimal payment schedule for your program.
- **Monitor Performance:** Track the impact of your payment schedule on affiliate performance and program success. Consider adjusting based on data.

- **Transparency:** Clearly communicate your payment schedule to your affiliates in your affiliate agreement.

**Additional Considerations:**

- **Affiliate Feedback:** Seek feedback from your affiliates on their preferences regarding payment timing.
- **Industry Standards:** Research common payment schedules in your niche to understand industry norms.

**Building a Sustainable Program:**

By implementing a well-defined payment schedule, minimizing chargeback risk, and offering ongoing value to your affiliates, you can create a program that fosters trust, incentivizes participation, and fuels growth for your online school.

Here are some additional tips for managing affiliate payments:

- **Automate Processes:** Automate affiliate payment processing to ensure efficiency and timely payouts.
- **Communicate Clearly:** Clearly communicate any changes to the payment schedule to your affiliates well in advance.
- **Track Payment History:** Maintain accurate records of affiliate payments made to ensure transparency and avoid disputes.

By implementing these strategies, you can move beyond simply setting a payment schedule and create a robust system that optimizes affiliate payouts, mitigates risk, and positions your program for long-term success.

## Supporting your affiliates with educational resources is crucial for a successful affiliate program. Here's a breakdown of the importance of affiliate education and some additional strategies:

**Empowering Your Affiliates:**

- **Content Creation Support:** Providing affiliates with content ideas, templates, and marketing materials reduces their workload and empowers them to promote your courses more effectively.
- **Industry Trends:** Educate your affiliates on current industry trends and best practices in affiliate marketing to help them optimize their promotional strategies.
- **Product Knowledge:** Ensure your affiliates have a deep understanding of your courses and their unique value propositions to create compelling marketing messages.

**Strategies for Affiliate Education:**

- **Affiliate Newsletter:** Create a dedicated newsletter for your affiliates filled with valuable content, including course updates, marketing tips, success stories, and industry insights.
- **Resource Library:** Develop a resource library with access to marketing materials, swipe copy, video templates, and other tools your affiliates can leverage.
- **Webinars and Training:** Host regular webinars or training sessions to educate your affiliates on your courses, promotional strategies, and best practices in affiliate marketing.

**Additional Considerations:**

- **Content Variety:** Offer a variety of educational resources in different formats (e.g., text, video, audio) to cater to different learning styles.
- **Regular Communication:** Maintain consistent communication with your affiliates to share new resources, updates, and industry trends.
- **Community Building:** Foster a sense of community among your affiliates by creating a forum or online space where they can connect, share ideas, and learn from each other.

**The Benefits of Education:**

- **Increased Engagement:** Educated affiliates are more engaged, confident, and effective at promoting your courses.
- **Improved Results:** Providing affiliate education can lead to increased sales conversions and program success.
- **Stronger Relationships:** Investing in affiliate education demonstrates your commitment to their success, strengthening your relationships with them.

**Scaling Your Approach:**

- **Frequency of Newsletters:** The frequency of your affiliate newsletter can be adjusted based on the volume of content you have to share.
- **Targeted Content:** Consider creating targeted content for different affiliate segments based on their experience or niche.

**Remember:**

Investing in affiliate education is an investment in the long-term success of your program. By empowering your affiliates with knowledge and resources, you can create a win-win situation for both your online school and your affiliate partners.

Here are some additional tips for educating your affiliates:

- **Gather Feedback:** Seek feedback from your affiliates on the types of educational resources they find most valuable.
- **Track Performance:** Monitor the impact of your affiliate education initiatives on program performance and adjust your strategy as needed.
- **Showcase Success Stories:** Feature success stories of top-performing affiliates to inspire and motivate others

Offering bonuses and incentives is a fantastic way to motivate your affiliates and make them feel valued members of your online school's community. Here's a breakdown of the importance of incentives and some creative ideas to consider:

**The Power of Incentives:**

- **Increased Motivation:** Bonuses and incentives can significantly boost affiliate motivation, leading to increased promotional efforts and sales for your courses.

- **A Sense of Value:** Incentives demonstrate that you appreciate your affiliates' contributions and are invested in their success.

- **Building Loyalty:** Well-designed incentive programs can foster long-term loyalty and commitment from your affiliates.

**Creative Incentive Ideas:**

- **Performance-Based Bonuses:** Reward top-performing affiliates with additional commissions, tiered payouts, or exclusive bonuses based on sales or leads generated.

- **Referral Bonuses:** Offer incentives to affiliates for referring other affiliates to your program.

- **Free Course Access:** Provide affiliates with free access to some of your courses to enhance their product knowledge and promotional capabilities.

- **Content Creation Tools:** Offer access to relevant content creation tools or software that can help affiliates produce high-quality marketing materials.
- **Early Access to New Courses:** Give your top affiliates early access to new course launches so they can create buzz and drive initial sales.
- **Contests and Giveaways:** Host contests or giveaways with exciting prizes (e.g., free tools, travel vouchers) to create excitement and motivate participation.
- **Public Recognition:** Publicly acknowledge and reward top-performing affiliates through your newsletter, social media, or website to showcase their achievements.

## Additional Considerations:

- **Align with Goals:** Design your incentive program to align with your specific program goals (e.g., driving sales, promoting specific courses).
- **Track and Analyze:** Monitor the impact of your incentive program on affiliate performance and program success.
- **Variety and Flexibility:** Consider offering a variety of incentives to cater to different affiliate preferences and motivations.

## Beyond Bonuses:

While bonuses and incentives are powerful tools, don't solely rely on them. Focus on building strong relationships, offering ongoing support, and providing valuable resources to cultivate a thriving affiliate community.

## Remember:

A well-structured incentive program, combined with a commitment to building strong relationships, can significantly enhance your affiliate marketing efforts. By providing value and acknowledging their contributions, you can create a program that motivates your affiliates, drives sales, and fuels the growth of your online school.

Here are some additional tips for implementing a successful incentive program:

- **Clearly Communicate Incentives:** Clearly outline your incentive program details and eligibility criteria in your affiliate agreement.
- **Set Achievable Goals:** Set realistic and achievable goals for earning bonuses and incentives to maintain affiliate motivation.
- **Time-Bound Offers:** Consider implementing time-bound incentives to create a sense of urgency and encourage immediate action.

By implementing these strategies, you can design a creative and effective incentive program that positions your affiliate marketing program for long-term success.

## PROMOTION

**Affiliate marketing, like any successful partnership, requires consistent effort, open communication, and a willingness to adapt. Here's a breakdown of the key points and some additional considerations:**

### Building Strong Affiliate Relationships:

- **Long-Term Commitment:** Success in affiliate marketing is a marathon, not a sprint. Be prepared to invest time and effort in building long-term relationships with your affiliates.
- **Mutual Support:** A successful program fosters a sense of mutual support. Provide ongoing support to your affiliates, and be open to their feedback and suggestions.
- **Continuous Improvement:** Continuously evaluate your program, gather affiliate feedback, and adapt your strategies to optimize performance over time.

### The Initial Launch Phase:

- **Dedicated Effort:** The initial launch phase of your affiliate program requires dedicated effort to establish a strong foundation.
- **Recruiting Affiliates:** Develop a targeted strategy to recruit high-quality affiliates who align with your brand and target audience.
- **Testing and Optimization:** Be prepared to test different approaches, analyze data, and optimize your program based on results.

### The Importance of Communication:

- **Open Communication:** Maintain open communication channels with your affiliates. Regularly share updates, address concerns, and answer questions promptly.

- **Transparency:** Be transparent about your program details, commission structures, and performance expectations.
- **Feedback Mechanisms:** Establish clear mechanisms for affiliates to provide feedback and suggestions for improvement.

**Additional Considerations:**

- **Community Building:** Foster a sense of community among your affiliates by creating a forum or online space for them to connect, share ideas, and support each other.
- **Celebrate Successes:** Recognize and celebrate the achievements of your top-performing affiliates to show appreciation and motivate others.
- **Industry Engagement:** Stay engaged with the affiliate marketing industry by attending conferences, following industry publications, and learning from other successful programs.

**Remember:**

Affiliate marketing is a collaborative effort. By investing in building strong relationships with your affiliates, providing ongoing support, and continuously optimizing your program, you can create a thriving partnership that drives sales and fuels the growth of your online school.

Here are some additional tips for building strong affiliate relationships:

- **Personalize Communication:** Personalize your communication with affiliates to build stronger connections and demonstrate that you value them as individuals.
- **Be Responsive:** Respond promptly to affiliate inquiries and questions to show that you're committed to their success.
- **Show Appreciation:** Express your appreciation to your affiliates for their contributions to your program.

By implementing these strategies, you can move beyond a transactional relationship and cultivate a collaborative environment where both you and your affiliates can thrive.

Effective affiliate marketing materials need to resonate with both the affiliate's brand and their audience. Here's a breakdown of the key points and some additional considerations:

**Tailored Content for Affiliate Success:**

- **Audience Alignment:** Ensure your promotional materials are tailored to the specific audience each affiliate caters to for better reception and promotion.

- **Brand Consistency:** The materials should align with the affiliate's brand aesthetic and messaging to maintain a cohesive experience for their audience.

- **High-Quality Design:** Invest in creating professional-looking, visually appealing marketing materials that reflect your brand positively.

**The Affiliate Approval Test:**

- **Self-Evaluation:** Before sending materials to affiliates, ask yourself if you would share them on your own channels. This ensures they are high-quality and relevant.

- **Clarity and Simplicity:** Use clear, concise language and avoid jargon to ensure the message is easily understood by the target audience.

**Additional Considerations:**

- **Variety of Formats:** Offer a variety of promotional materials (e.g., banners, social media posts, email templates) to cater to different affiliate preferences.

- **Customization Options:** Consider providing customizable templates that affiliates can tailor to their brand and audience.

- **Easy Integration:** Make it easy for affiliates to integrate your promotional materials into their existing marketing efforts.

**Optimizing Your Approach:**

- **Affiliate Feedback:** Seek feedback from your affiliates on the types of promotional materials they find most useful and effective.
- **Data Tracking:** Track the performance of different promotional materials to identify what resonates best with your target audience.
- **Continuous Improvement:** Based on feedback and data, refine your promotional materials to achieve better results.

**Remember:**

High-quality, targeted promotional materials are essential for empowering your affiliates to promote your courses effectively. By investing in creating valuable content that aligns with their needs and audience, you can significantly boost the success of your affiliate marketing program.

Here are some additional tips for creating effective affiliate marketing materials:

- **Highlight Value Propositions:** Focus on the key benefits and value propositions of your courses in your promotional materials.
- **Target Pain Points:** Address the pain points and challenges faced by your target audience to demonstrate how your courses offer solutions.
- **Strong Call to Action:** Include a clear and compelling call to action (e.g., "Enroll Now") to encourage conversions.

By implementing these strategies, you can create a library of effective affiliate marketing materials that empower your partners and drive sales for your online school.

Effective communication is crucial for building strong relationships with your affiliates. While online tools can be helpful, consider these additional strategies to go beyond the standard methods:

**Moving Beyond Traditional Communication:**

- **Multi-Channel Approach:** Utilize a variety of communication channels (e.g., email, social media, instant messaging) to cater to different affiliate preferences.
- **Personalized Communication:** Personalize your communication with affiliates to build rapport and demonstrate you value them as individuals.
- **Focus on Relationship Building:** Move beyond transactional communication and engage in conversations that build trust and understanding.

**Exploring Innovative Approaches:**

- **Webinars and Live Events:** Host regular webinars or live events to educate affiliates, share updates, and answer questions in real-time.
- **One-on-One Calls:** Schedule regular one-on-one calls with your top affiliates to discuss performance, address concerns, and offer personalized support.
- **Affiliate Advisory Board:** Consider forming an affiliate advisory board to gather feedback, brainstorm ideas, and foster a sense of community.
- **Social Media Groups:** Create private social media groups for affiliates to connect, share ideas, and support each other in a more informal setting.

### Choosing the Right Channels:

- **Affiliate Feedback:** Seek feedback from your affiliates on their preferred communication channels and styles.
- **Track Engagement:** Monitor which communication channels generate the most engagement and adapt your strategy accordingly.
- **Experimentation:** Don't be afraid to experiment with different communication methods to discover what works best for your program and your affiliates.

### The Benefits of Strong Communication:

- **Increased Engagement:** Strong communication fosters a sense of community and encourages affiliate participation.
- **Improved Performance:** Effective communication can lead to better affiliate performance through education, motivation, and problem-solving.
- **Stronger Relationships:** Investing in communication builds trust, loyalty, and long-term partnerships with your affiliates.

### Remember:

The best communication methods are those that foster open dialogue, build trust, and empower your affiliates. By being flexible, innovative, and responsive, you can establish a communication strategy that positions your affiliate program for long-term success.

Here are some additional tips for communicating effectively with your affiliates:

- **Respond Promptly:** Strive to respond to affiliate inquiries and questions promptly to demonstrate your commitment to their success.
- **Be Transparent:** Maintain transparent communication by sharing relevant program updates, performance data, and industry insights.
- **Show Appreciation:** Express your gratitude to your affiliates for their contributions to your program.

By implementing these strategies, you can move beyond basic communication and create a collaborative environment where your affiliates feel valued and supported.

# TERMS AND CONDITIONS

A well-defined affiliate program agreement is crucial for establishing a strong legal foundation and clear expectations for both you and your affiliates. Here's a breakdown of the key points and some additional considerations:

**The Importance of Affiliate Program Agreements:**

- **Legal Framework:** A formal agreement outlines the terms and conditions of your program, protecting both you and your affiliates.
- **Clear Expectations:** The agreement defines acceptable behavior, commission structures, and responsibilities for both parties.
- **Dispute Resolution:** A well-defined agreement establishes guidelines for resolving potential disputes or misunderstandings.

**Essential Components of an Affiliate Agreement:**

- **Program Overview:** Clearly outline the purpose and goals of your affiliate program.

- **Eligibility Requirements:** Specify the criteria for affiliates to join your program.

- **Commission Structure:** Define the commission rates or payment terms for affiliates.

- **Tracking and Reporting:** Explain how affiliate sales and performance will be tracked and reported.

- Transparency around core program details is essential for attracting and retaining high-quality affiliates. Here's a breakdown of the key information you should include in your affiliate program agreement:

**Commission Structure:**

- **Rates:** Clearly outline your commission rates (percentage of sale or flat fee) for different products or course offerings.

- **Payment Timing:** Specify when commissions are awarded (e.g., after refund period ends). Consider a common timeframe like "30 days after the end of the refund period."

- **Restrictions and Exceptions:** Define any limitations on commission eligibility (e.g., product categories, minimum sales thresholds).

- **Coupon Usage:** Explain how coupon usage impacts commissions (e.g., commissions based on discounted price or full price).

**Affiliate Tracking and Payment:**

- **Cookie Duration:** Specify the duration for which your affiliate tracking system stores cookies in users' browsers (e.g., 30 days, 90 days).

- **Data Privacy:** Link to your detailed cookie consent and data privacy policy documents for affiliates to review.

- **Data Storage:** Explain what data you store about affiliates (e.g., contact information, performance metrics) and where it's stored.

- **Payment Schedule:** Outline your payment schedule (e.g., monthly) and preferred payout methods (e.g., PayPal, bank transfer).

**Additional Considerations:**

- **Clear Language:** Use clear and concise language to ensure all terms and conditions are easily understood by your affiliates.

- **Accessibility:** Make the affiliate program agreement readily available on your website for easy access and review.

- **Updates:** Periodically review and update your agreement to reflect any changes in your program or legal requirements.

Here's an example of how you might structure this section in your agreement:

**Commission Structure:**

- **Commission Rate:** You will earn a commission of [percentage]% for each sale of our [course name] product referred through your unique affiliate link.
- **Payment Timing:** Commissions are awarded 30 days after the end of the refund period for the purchased product.
- **Restrictions and Exceptions:** Commissions are not awarded for sales generated through coupon codes not provided by us.

**Affiliate Tracking and Payment:**

- **Cookie Duration:** Our affiliate tracking system stores cookies in users' browsers for 30 days.
- **Data Privacy:** Please refer to our detailed Cookie Consent Policy and Data Privacy Policy for more information (link to documents).
- **Data Storage:** We store your contact information, performance metrics (e.g., sales generated), and any communication history with us. All data is stored securely on our servers.
- **Payment Schedule:** We process affiliate payouts on a monthly basis via PayPal.

By providing clear and detailed information about your program structure, tracking system, and payment methods, you can establish trust and transparency with your affiliates, fostering a successful and long-lasting partnership.

# Outlining clear guidelines for brand representation and affiliate conduct is crucial for protecting both your brand and your affiliates. Here's a breakdown of the key points and some additional considerations to include in your affiliate program agreement:

**Brand Representation:**

- **Logo Usage:** Provide specific instructions on how affiliates can use your logo (e.g., size, color variations).
- **Brand Name:** Outline any guidelines regarding the use of your brand name in marketing materials.
- **Affiliate Disclosure:** Require clear and conspicuous disclosure of the affiliate relationship with your company, following FTC guidelines (explained below).

**Promotional Materials:**

- **Landing Pages and Resources:** If you provide specific landing pages or promotional materials, make them readily available to affiliates.
- **Paid Advertising:** Specify your policy on paid advertising (e.g., allowed platforms, restrictions on targeting or messaging).

**Affiliate Disclosures and FTC Regulations:**

- **Global Compliance:** For operations outside the US, mention the need to comply with local regulations regarding affiliate disclosures.

- **FTC Disclosure Requirements:** Explain the FTC's affiliate disclosure requirements (e.g., clear and conspicuous disclosure in all online mediums).
- **Disclosure Examples:** Consider providing examples of compliant disclosures to guide your affiliates.

**Additional Considerations:**

- **Content Standards:** You may consider including optional content standards if you have specific quality expectations for affiliate promotions.

**Here's an example of how you might structure this section in your agreement:**

**Brand Representation:**

- **Logo Usage:** Affiliates are permitted to use our official logo as displayed on our brand assets page. Any modifications to the logo require prior written approval.
- **Brand Name:** The [Your Company Name] brand name should be used accurately and respectfully in all promotional materials.
- **Affiliate Disclosure:** All affiliates are required to disclose their affiliate relationship with [Your Company Name] conspicuously in accordance with FTC guidelines.

**Promotional Materials:**

- **Landing Pages and Resources:** A library of approved landing pages and promotional materials is available for affiliates in the affiliate portal.
- **Paid Advertising:** Paid advertising to promote our courses is permitted on most major platforms, but affiliates must comply with our advertising guidelines (link to guidelines).

**Affiliate Disclosures and FTC Regulations:**

- **Global Compliance:** Affiliates operating outside the US are responsible for complying with all local affiliate disclosure regulations.
- **FTC Disclosure Requirements:** In accordance with FTC guidelines, affiliates must clearly and conspicuously disclose their affiliate relationship with [Your Company Name] in all online mediums where they promote our products or services. This includes web pages, articles, blog posts, social media posts, videos, webinars, podcasts, ebooks, illustrations, and infographics. Banner ads do not require disclosure.

By establishing clear expectations for brand representation, promotional activities, and affiliate disclosures, you can protect your brand reputation, ensure your affiliates comply with regulations, and foster a healthy partnership environment.

# MY BUSINESS

ffiliate marketing offers a powerful strategy for online schools to reach new audiences and expand their reach. Here's a breakdown of the key points and some additional considerations:

## The Power of Affiliate Marketing for Online Schools:

- **Targeted Audience Reach:** Leverage affiliates with audiences that align with your ideal student profile for efficient marketing.
- **Growing Online Education Market:** The increasing demand for online education (e.g., +10% annually as per Technavio studies) creates a fertile ground for your courses.
- **Performance-Based Growth:** Affiliate marketing allows you to focus resources on successful affiliates who drive sales.

## Factors Affecting Success:

- **Affiliate Quality:** Recruiting high-quality affiliates with engaged audiences is crucial for program success.
- **Direct Promotion:** Prioritize affiliates who actively promote your school and courses to their audience.
- **Patience and Investment:** Building a successful affiliate program requires patience, consistent effort, and marketing resource allocation.

## Strategies for Faster Growth:

- **Targeted Recruitment:** Identify and recruit affiliates who cater to specific demographics or interests relevant to your courses.
- **Incentive Programs:** Implement effective incentive programs (bonuses, rewards) to motivate affiliates and drive sales.
- **High-Quality Resources:** Provide affiliates with valuable resources (e.g., marketing materials, training) to empower their promotions.
- **Performance Tracking:** Monitor affiliate performance data to identify top performers and optimize your program.
- **Communication and Support:** Maintain open communication with affiliates, address their concerns, and offer ongoing support.

## Additional Considerations:

- **Niche Expertise:** Consider partnering with micro-influencers or niche-specific affiliates who have a loyal following.

- **Content Marketing:** Encourage affiliates to create valuable content (e.g., blog posts, reviews) that showcase your courses.
- **Community Building:** Foster a community among your affiliates for knowledge sharing, collaboration, and mutual support.

By implementing these strategies, you can build a robust affiliate marketing program that fuels the growth of your online school. Remember, success takes time and effort, but with a well-defined approach, you can leverage the power of affiliate marketing to reach a wider audience and achieve your enrollment goals.

The growth trajectory of affiliate marketing programs can vary significantly. Here's a breakdown of the factors influencing growth and some additional considerations:

**Factors Affecting Affiliate Program Growth:**

- **Program Design:** A well-structured program with clear goals, attractive incentives, and valuable resources fosters faster growth.
- **Affiliate Quality:** Recruiting high-quality affiliates with engaged and relevant audiences is crucial for driving sales.
- **Marketing Efforts:** Consistent promotion of your program, both internally and through affiliates, accelerates program awareness.
- **Market Saturation:** The competitiveness of your niche and the number of existing affiliate programs can impact growth speed.
- **External Factors:** Economic trends and industry changes can influence consumer behavior and affiliate marketing results.

**The Power of Patience and Persistence:**

- **Realistic Expectations:** Allow sufficient time (at least a year) for your program to gain traction and attract high-performing affiliates.
- **Focus on Long-Term Growth:** Building a sustainable affiliate program requires ongoing effort, optimization, and relationship building.

**The Impact of Influencers:**

- **High ROI Potential:** Partnering with a large influencer or a highly effective affiliate can significantly improve your program's return on investment (ROI).
- **Targeted Reach:** Influencers with a strong connection to your target audience can generate a surge in qualified leads and conversions.

**Additional Considerations:**

- **Tracking and Analysis:** Continuously monitor affiliate program performance data to identify areas for improvement and optimize your strategy.
- **Affiliate Feedback:** Seek feedback from your affiliates to understand their needs and adapt your program accordingly.
- **Testing and Experimentation:** Don't be afraid to test different approaches (e.g., commission structures, marketing channels) to discover what works best.

**Remember:**

Affiliate marketing is a marathon, not a sprint. By investing in a well-designed program, fostering strong affiliate relationships, and adapting to changing trends, you can build a sustainable affiliate marketing program that delivers long-term success for your online school.

Here are some additional tips for accelerating your affiliate program's growth:

- **Case Studies and Testimonials:** Showcase the success stories of your top-performing affiliates to inspire and motivate others.
- **Affiliate Contests and Challenges:** Host contests or challenges with exciting rewards to incentivize affiliate participation and sales generation.
- **Industry Events and Conferences:** Attend industry events and conferences to network with potential affiliates and build brand awareness.

By implementing these strategies and maintaining a patient and persistent approach, you can increase your chances of achieving significant growth within your affiliate marketing program.

That's right! Having a well-defined affiliate program agreement is essential for establishing a strong foundation for your program. It outlines the rights and responsibilities of both you and your affiliates, fostering trust and transparency in the partnership.

Here's a breakdown of the key steps you should take:

1. **Access the Affiliate Agreement Template:** Click the "Edit page" button to access the pre-built affiliate program agreement template.
2. **Review the Terms and Conditions:** Carefully read through the provided template to understand the standard terms and conditions governing the program.
3. **Customize the Agreement:** Review each section of the agreement and make any necessary adjustments to reflect your specific program details, such as:

- Commission structure (rates, payout timing)
- Affiliate tracking and payment methods (cookie duration, data storage)

- Brand representation guidelines (logo usage, brand name)
- Promotional material allowances (landing pages, paid advertising)
- Termination clauses (grounds for termination for both parties)

4. **Save Your Agreement:** Once you've made your customizations, hit the "Save" button to finalize your affiliate program agreement.

**Additional Considerations:**

- **Seek Legal Counsel:** While the template provides a helpful starting point, consider consulting with a legal professional to ensure the agreement complies with all relevant laws and regulations.

- **Clarity and Accessibility:** Use clear and concise language throughout the agreement to ensure easy understanding for both you and your affiliates.

- **Maintain a Copy:** Keep a copy of your finalized affiliate program agreement readily available for your records and for reference by your affiliates.

By following these steps and leveraging the provided template, you can save time and effort while creating a comprehensive and legally sound affiliate program agreement that sets your program up for success.

Do you have any other questions about affiliate marketing or your online school? I'm happy to assist you further.

# The commission rate you offer is a crucial element in attracting and retaining high-quality affiliates for your online school's affiliate program. Here's a breakdown of what to consider when setting your commission rate:

**Understanding Commission Rates:**
•**Industry Standards:** Research commission rates offered by similar online schools and affiliate programs within your niche to establish a benchmark.
•**Product Value:** Consider the value of your courses and the typical price point when determining a suitable commission rate.
•**Affiliate Effort:** Factor in the effort required from affiliates to promote your courses effectively (e.g., content creation, marketing activities).
•**Program Goals:** Align your commission rate with your program goals. If you prioritize rapid growth, a higher rate might be attractive.
**The Range of Commission Rates:**
•**Typical Range:** As you mentioned, commission rates typically range between 10% and 50% of the product sale price.
•**Factors Influencing Range:** The specific rate within this range depends on the factors mentioned above (industry, product value, affiliate effort).
**The Power of Choice:**

- **Competitive Advantage:** Offering a competitive commission rate can attract more affiliates and incentivize them to promote your courses actively.
- **Profitability:** Ensure your chosen commission rate allows you to maintain profitability after accounting for course creation costs, marketing expenses, and affiliate payouts.

**Beyond Commission Rates:**

- **Tiered Commissions:** Consider implementing a tiered commission structure where rates increase based on sales volume achieved by the affiliate.
- **Performance Bonuses:** Offer additional bonuses for top-performing affiliates to further incentivize strong sales efforts.
- **Promotional Resources:** Provide valuable promotional materials and resources to empower affiliates and potentially offset lower commission rates.

**Finding the Right Balance:**

The ideal commission rate for your program depends on your specific circumstances and goals. By carefully considering the factors mentioned above, you can establish a rate that attracts high-quality affiliates, motivates strong promotion, and ensures the long-term sustainability of your program. Here are some additional tips for setting your commission rate:

- **Gather Affiliate Feedback:** Seek input from potential or existing affiliates to understand their expectations regarding commission rates.
- **Track and Analyze Performance:** Monitor the impact of your commission rate on affiliate recruitment and sales performance.
- **Be Flexible and Adaptable:** Be prepared to adjust your commission rate over time based on program performance and market trends.

By implementing these strategies, you can find the optimal commission rate that positions your affiliate program for success and fosters mutually beneficial partnerships with your affiliates.

You've absolutely nailed the concept of affiliate cookie expiration and commission payout tied to refund policies! Here's a breakdown of the key points and some additional considerations:

**Affiliate Cookie Expiration:**

- **Tracking Referrals:** Cookies with an appropriate expiration period (15-60 days) ensure affiliates receive credit for referrals within that timeframe.

- **Optimal Duration:** Balancing the window for potential customer conversion with data privacy concerns is crucial.

**Commission Payout and Refunds:**

- **Refund Policy:** The timeframe for your refund policy determines when commissions become payable to affiliates.

- **Holding Period:** Consider implementing a holding period (e.g., 30 days after purchase) before paying commissions to account for potential refunds.

**Example Scenario:**

- **Cookie Expiration:** 60-day cookie.

- **Refund Policy:** 30-day full refund window.

- **Commission Payout:** Affiliates would receive commission for sales only after the 30-day refund period has passed, ensuring the customer doesn't request a refund.

**Additional Considerations:**

- **Transparency:** Clearly communicate your cookie expiration period and commission payout policy to affiliates in your program agreement.
- **Data Privacy:** Ensure compliance with data privacy regulations regarding cookie usage and customer tracking.
- **Affiliate Communication:** Keep affiliates informed about any changes to your cookie expiration or commission payout policy.

**Optimizing Your Approach:**

- **Data Analysis:** Monitor your program's performance data to identify the optimal cookie expiration duration for your audience and conversion rates.
- **Affiliate Feedback:** Seek feedback from affiliates regarding their experience with the current cookie expiration period.

By implementing these strategies, you can establish a fair and efficient system for tracking referrals, awarding commissions, and managing refunds within your affiliate program.

Here are some additional tips for managing cookie expiration and commission payouts:

- **Tiered Commissions:** Consider a tiered payout structure where a portion of the commission is paid upfront and the remaining balance is paid after the refund period.
- **Affiliate Portal:** Provide a user-friendly affiliate portal where affiliates can track their referrals, commission earnings, and payout status.
- **Clear Communication:** Maintain open communication with affiliates to address any questions or concerns they might have regarding cookie expiration and commission payouts.

By following these recommendations, you can create a well-structured system that fosters trust and transparency with your affiliates while protecting your business interests.

# PAGE SETTING

A well-designed affiliate registration page is a crucial element for attracting and onboarding potential partners to your online school's affiliate program. Here's a breakdown of the key points and some additional considerations:

### The Importance of the Affiliate Registration Page:

- **First Impression:** The registration page serves as the first point of contact for potential affiliates and shapes their initial impression of your program.
- **Clear Communication:** Clearly explain the value proposition of your program, the benefits of becoming an affiliate, and the signup process.
- **Streamlined Registration:** Ensure the registration process is user-friendly, with minimal steps and clear instructions to encourage signups.

### Leveraging Your Page Builder:

- **Customization:** Utilize the page builder's features to create a visually appealing and informative registration page that aligns with your brand identity.
- **Call to Action:** Include a strong call to action button that encourages users to sign up for your affiliate program.
- **Integrations:** Explore integrating your page builder with your affiliate management system for seamless data flow and user experience.

### Beyond the Registration Page:

- **Affiliate Dashboard:** Design a user-friendly and informative affiliate dashboard where affiliates can access essential information, track performance, and manage their accounts.
- **Multiple Access Points:** Provide access to the affiliate dashboard through various methods, such as the affiliate registration page button and user profile links.
- **Manual Affiliate Addition:** Offer the option for manually adding trusted users as affiliates through your user management system.

### Additional Considerations:

- **Targeted Content:** Tailor the registration page content to resonate with your ideal affiliate profile.
- **Benefits and Incentives:** Highlight the benefits and incentives offered to affiliates to attract high-quality partners.
- **Transparency and Trust:** Maintain transparency throughout the registration process and build trust with potential affiliates.

By creating a well-designed registration page, a user-friendly affiliate dashboard, and flexible signup options, you can streamline the onboarding process and nurture strong relationships with your affiliates from the very beginning.

Here are some additional tips for optimizing your affiliate registration process:

- **Pre-Filled Forms (Optional):** Consider pre-filling certain fields (e.g., website URL) with publicly available data to reduce signup time.
- **Welcome Email:** Send a personalized welcome email to new affiliates with program information, resources, and next steps.

- **Ongoing Communication:** Maintain open communication with affiliates to address their questions and provide ongoing support.

By implementing these strategies, you can attract top-tier affiliates, simplify onboarding, and set your affiliate program up for long-term success.

Customizing the affiliate dashboard view within your program settings is essential for providing affiliates with relevant and actionable information. Here's a breakdown of the key points and some additional considerations:

## The Affiliate Dashboard: A Window into Performance

- **Information Hub:** The affiliate dashboard serves as a central location for affiliates to access key performance metrics, track earnings, and manage their accounts.

- **Customizable Views:** The ability to control what information affiliates see empowers you to tailor the dashboard to their needs.

- **Transparency and Motivation:** Providing clear and transparent data on commissions can motivate affiliates and encourage continued promotion efforts.

## Commission Visibility Options:

- **All Commissions:** This option grants affiliates a comprehensive view of all earned commissions, regardless of payout status.

- **Approved Commissions:** This option shows commissions that have been approved but haven't yet reached the payout timeframe.

- **Payable Commissions:** This option displays commissions that are ready for payout after the refund or maturation period has passed.

- **Paid Commissions:** This option shows commissions that have already been paid out to the affiliate.

## Benefits of Customization:

- **Targeted Information:** Providing affiliates with the most relevant commission data (e.g., payable commissions) helps them focus on optimizing their promotional efforts for immediate rewards.

- **Performance Tracking:** Enabling access to all commissions allows affiliates to track their overall performance and identify areas for improvement.

- **Transparency and Trust:** Transparency regarding commission status fosters trust and strengthens your relationship with your affiliates.

## Beyond Commission Visibility:

- **Additional Metrics:** Consider including other valuable metrics in the dashboard, such as clicks, conversions, and referral traffic.

- **Data Visualization:** Present data in an easy-to-understand format with charts, graphs, or visual elements to enhance comprehension.

- **Downloadable Reports:** Allow affiliates to download detailed reports for their records and further analysis.

**Additional Considerations:**

- **Affiliate Feedback:** Seek feedback from your affiliates regarding the information they find most valuable on the dashboard.
- **Regular Updates:** Ensure timely updates to commission data and other metrics within the affiliate dashboard.
- **User Experience:** Prioritize user experience by creating a clean, intuitive, and easy-to-navigate affiliate dashboard.

By providing a customizable and informative affiliate dashboard, you empower your affiliates with the insights they need to make informed decisions and optimize their promotional strategies. This transparency and data access can contribute significantly to the success of your affiliate program.

Do you have any other questions about affiliate program settings or dashboard functionalities? I'm happy to assist you further.

Offering a variety of convenient payout options is essential for attracting and retaining high-quality affiliates for your online school's affiliate program. Here's a breakdown of the available options and some additional considerations:

**Affiliate Payout Options:**

- **Convenience and Flexibility:** Providing multiple payout methods caters to the preferences of diverse affiliates and ensures they receive their commissions efficiently.
- **Popular Options:** PayPal and bank transfers are widely used and trusted payout methods for affiliate programs.
- **Considering "Other":** Enabling an "Other" option with a text field allows affiliates to specify alternative payout methods they might prefer.

**Benefits of Multiple Payout Options:**

- **Increased Affiliate Satisfaction:** Offering a variety of payout choices demonstrates your commitment to affiliate satisfaction and simplifies the commission receiving process.
- **Reduced Friction:** By accommodating different preferences, you minimize potential roadblocks for affiliates to receive their earnings.
- **Global Considerations:** If your program attracts international affiliates, research popular payout methods in their respective regions.

**Managing the "Other" Option:**

- **Clear Communication:** If you enable the "Other" option, clearly communicate any limitations or additional requirements for alternative payout methods.

- **Affiliate Expertise:** Align course selection with the expertise and target audience of your ideal affiliates to maximize promotion effectiveness.
- **Performance Tracking:** Monitor which courses generate the most sales through affiliate promotions to optimize your course selection over time.

### Additional Considerations:

- **Course Bundles:** If you offer course bundles, determine whether the entire bundle or individual courses within it will be available for affiliate promotion.
- **Course Updates:** Ensure that courses included in your affiliate program are up-to-date and reflect the latest information in your field.
- **Affiliate Communication:** Clearly communicate the list of courses available for affiliate promotion within your program agreement and the affiliate dashboard.

### Pro Tip: Leverage Automation

- Consider exploring automation tools that can simplify the process of adding new courses to your affiliate program as you create them.

By strategically selecting courses for affiliate promotion, you can ensure your affiliates have the most relevant and profitable offerings to showcase to their audiences. This targeted approach can significantly benefit both your affiliates' success and your program's overall growth.

A robust affiliate management system with real-time reporting is essential for monitoring the success of your online school's affiliate program. Here's a breakdown of the key functionalities you mentioned and some additional considerations:

### Affiliate Management Dashboard:

- **Real-Time Insights:** The ability to access real-time data empowers you to track program performance, identify trends, and make informed decisions.
- **Dedicated Sections:** Having separate pages for Affiliates, Rewards/Commissions, Payouts, Leads, and Customers provides a clear and organized view of all program aspects.
- **Benefits of Each Section:**
- **Affiliates:** Track affiliate activity, performance metrics, and manage their accounts.
- **Rewards/Commissions:** Monitor commission structures, earned commissions, and payout details.
- **Payouts:** Manage and track affiliate payouts, ensuring timely and accurate payments.
- **Leads:** Analyze lead generation data to understand your affiliate program's effectiveness in driving potential customers.
- **Customers:** Gain insights into customer acquisition through affiliate promotions and track customer

- **Review and Approval Process:** Establish a process to review and approve alternative payout me
  before processing commissions.
- **Security and Compliance:** Ensure that any alternative payout methods comply with relevant secur
  and financial regulations.

**Additional Considerations:**

- **Minimum Payout Threshold:** Consider setting a minimum payout threshold to manage administrativ
  costs associated with frequent, low-value payouts.
- **Payout Schedule:** Clearly define your payout schedule (e.g., monthly, bi-weekly) and ensure timely
  processing of commissions.
- **Transparency:** Communicate your payout options and policies clearly within your affiliate program
  agreement and the affiliate dashboard.

By offering a variety of convenient and reliable payout options, you can enhance the overall experience
for your affiliates and foster a thriving affiliate program for your online school.

Here are some additional tips for managing affiliate payouts:

- **Automated Payouts:** Explore integrating your affiliate program with automated payout systems to
  streamline the process.
- **Payment Receipts:** Provide affiliates with clear payment receipts for each commission payout.
- **Affiliate Communication:** Keep affiliates informed about the status of their commissions and any
  upcoming payouts.

By implementing these strategies, you can ensure smooth and efficient affiliate payouts, building trust
and loyalty within your program.

That's a crucial detail to remember when setting up your affiliate program! Here's a breakdown of the
key points and some additional considerations regarding course selection for affiliate promotions:

**Specifying Courses for Affiliate Marketing:**

- **Inclusion Control:** The ability to choose which courses and bundles are included in your affiliate
  program empowers you to strategically align your offerings with affiliate promotion efforts.
- **Promoting the Right Courses:** Focus on including courses that are relevant to your ideal affiliates'
  audiences and hold high income potential for both you and your affiliates.
- **Paid Courses Only:** Affiliate marketing is typically suited for paid courses, as commissions are
  generated from sales. Free or private courses wouldn't provide a commission opportunity.

**Making Informed Choices:**

- **Course Value:** Consider the value proposition and price point of each course when deciding on its
  inclusion in the affiliate program.

behavior.

**Additional Considerations:**

- **Data Visualization:** Utilize charts, graphs, and other visual elements to enhance data comprehension and identify trends quickly.

- **Customizable Reports:** Allow affiliates (and yourself) to generate custom reports based on specific timeframes or performance metrics.

- **Exporting Data:** Enable data export for further analysis in external tools if needed.

- **Performance Benchmarks:** Establish performance benchmarks to track your program's progress and identify areas for improvement.

**Leveraging Insights for Growth:**

By analyzing the data available within your affiliate management system, you can:

- **Identify Top-Performing Affiliates:** Recognize and reward high-performing affiliates to incentivize continued success.

- **Optimize Campaign Strategies:** Tailor your marketing efforts to support effective affiliate promotion of specific courses.

- **Refine Commission Structures:** Adjust commission rates or structures based on performance data to maximize program profitability.

- **Identify Growth Opportunities:** Uncover areas where your program can be improved to attract more affiliates and drive sales.

**Remember:**

Data is your friend in affiliate marketing. By effectively utilizing the insights provided by your affiliate management system, you can make data-driven decisions to optimize your program and achieve sustainable growth for your online school.

The "Affiliates" section within your affiliate management system is a vital hub for managing your relationships with your program's partners. Here's a breakdown of the functionalities you described and some additional considerations:

### The "Affiliates" Section: A Gateway to Affiliate Management
•**Affiliate List:** This section provides a comprehensive overview of all your affiliates, including essential details like contact information, performance metrics, and commission information.
•**Manual Affiliate Addition:** The ability to manually add affiliates allows you to recruit specific partners who align well with your brand and target audience.
•**Key Affiliate Details:**
•**Contact Information:** Email addresses are crucial for communication with your affiliates.
•**Customer Acquisition:** Track the number of customers each affiliate brings in to assess their promotional effectiveness.
•**Sales Performance:** Monitor affiliate sales data to identify top performers and optimize your program accordingly.

- **Commission Rate:** View the agreed-upon commission rate for each affiliate.
- **Financial Tracking:** Keep track of outstanding commissions owed to each affiliate and payments already made.

## Affiliate User Profiles:

- **Detailed Performance Insights:** By clicking on an affiliate's profile, you can delve deeper into their performance data, gaining a granular understanding of their contribution to your program.
- **Specific Metrics:**
- **Affiliate ID:** A unique identifier for each affiliate.
- **Payment Method:** The method chosen by the affiliate to receive their commissions.
- **Referral Tracking:** Monitor clicks on the affiliate's referral link and track leads generated.
- **Sales and Commissions:** Analyze individual affiliate sales figures and corresponding commission amounts.
- **Payment History:** Track the payout schedule and view past commission payments made to each affiliate.

## Benefits of Effective Affiliate Management:

- **Stronger Affiliate Relationships:** Maintaining clear communication and providing performance insights fosters trust and strengthens your relationships with affiliates.
- **Data-Driven Decisions:** Access to detailed affiliate performance data empowers you to make informed decisions regarding commission structures, marketing strategies, and program optimization.
- **Identifying Growth Opportunities:** By analyzing affiliate performance, you can identify successful strategies and replicate them to further grow your program.

## Additional Considerations:

- **Search and Filter Options:** Utilize search and filter functions within the "Affiliates" section to easily find specific affiliates based on various criteria.
- **Performance Notes:** Consider incorporating a notes section in affiliate profiles to track communication history or relevant details about each affiliate.
- **Affiliate Communication Tools:** Explore built-in communication tools within your affiliate management system to streamline communication with your affiliates.

By effectively managing your affiliates and leveraging the insights offered by the "Affiliates" section, you can cultivate a thriving affiliate network that fuels the growth of your online school.

The ability to manually add affiliates is a valuable feature for strategically recruiting partners who are a good fit for your online school's affiliate program. Here's a breakdown of the process and some additional considerations:

## Manual Affiliate Addition: A Targeted Approach

- **Strategic Recruitment:** Manual addition allows you to target specific users who demonstrate potential as successful affiliates, such as existing students or engaged community members.

- **User Requirement:** As you mentioned, the user you want to add as an affiliate must already be registered with your online school.

- **Simple Process:** The "Add Affiliate" button typically initiates a straightforward process for adding new affiliates manually.

## Additional Considerations:

- **Selection Criteria:** Establish clear criteria for identifying potential affiliates who can effectively promote your courses and reach your target audience.

- **Communication and Consent:** Before manually adding someone as an affiliate, reach out to them to explain the program, answer their questions, and obtain their consent.
- **Affiliate Agreement:** Ensure new affiliates (manual or self-registered) understand and agree to the terms and conditions outlined in your affiliate program agreement.

**Optimizing Your Manual Recruitment:**

- **Targeted Invitations:** Consider offering exclusive benefits or incentives to existing users you invite to join your affiliate program.
- **Onboarding Process:** Provide new affiliates with onboarding resources, training materials, and marketing tools to empower their promotional efforts.
- **Ongoing Support:** Establish clear communication channels and offer ongoing support to your affiliates to address their questions and concerns.

By strategically recruiting and effectively onboarding manual affiliates, you can cultivate a network of highly motivated partners who are invested in the success of your program.

Here are some additional tips for optimizing your manual affiliate recruitment:

- **Affiliate Contests and Incentives:** Organize contests or offer rewards for top-performing manual affiliates to drive program participation.
- **Affiliate Testimonials:** Showcase success stories of existing manual affiliates to inspire and motivate potential new partners.
- **Track Manual Affiliate Performance:** Monitor the performance of manually added affiliates to assess the effectiveness of your recruitment strategy.

By implementing these strategies, you can leverage manual affiliate addition to build a targeted and successful affiliate network for your online school.

The "Commissions" section within your affiliate management system is a vital tool for tracking, managing, and processing affiliate commissions within your online school's program. Here's a breakdown of the functionalities you described and some additional considerations:

**The "Commissions" Section: A Hub for Commission Management**

- **Comprehensive Overview:** This section provides a detailed breakdown of all commissions generated through your affiliate program, including individual sales details and payout statuses.
- **Financial Transparency:** Being able to directly see what you owe or have paid to each affiliate fosters transparency and builds trust within your program.
- **Key Commission Details:**
- **Sales Performance:** Track commission amounts associated with each sale generated by an affiliate.

- **Purchase Dates:** Monitor the dates of purchases linked to each commission, enabling you to track sales trends.
- **Payment Status:** View the current status of each commission (pending, approved, rejected, paid).
- **Approval and Rejection Control:** The ability to approve or reject commissions offers flexibility in managing your program and addressing potential discrepancies.
- **Organized Tabs:** The presence of separate tabs for "Accepted," "Rejected," "Due," and "Paid" commissions allows for easy filtering and streamlined management.

**Benefits of Effective Commission Management:**

- **Accurate Payouts:** Ensures timely and accurate payout of commissions to your affiliates, fostering positive program relationships.
- **Fraud Prevention:** The ability to review and approve commissions offers a layer of control to prevent fraudulent activity within your program.
- **Data-Driven Decisions:** Analyzing commission data can help you identify top-performing affiliates, optimize commission structures, and track program profitability.

**Additional Considerations:**

- **Automated Commission Calculation:** Integrate automation tools to avoid manual calculations and ensure accuracy in commission processing.
- **Clear Commission Approval Criteria:** Establish clear and transparent criteria for approving or rejecting commissions to maintain consistency and fairness.
- **Communication During Rejections:** If a commission is rejected, communicate the reason clearly and promptly to the affected affiliate.
- **Payment Schedule Transparency:** Clearly communicate your payout schedule to affiliates so they understand when to expect commission payments.

**Pro Tip: Automate Where Possible**

Explore automation tools that can streamline commission calculations, approvals, and payouts within your affiliate program. This can save you time and minimize errors in the commission management process.

By effectively managing commissions through the dedicated section, you can ensure accurate and timely payments to your affiliates while maintaining program integrity. This builds trust and fosters long-term success for your online school's affiliate program.

The "Payments" section of your affiliate management system is crucial for managing affiliate program payouts efficiently. Here's a breakdown of the functionalities you described and some additional considerations:

### The "Payments" Section: Streamlining Affiliate Payouts

- **Payout Management:** This section provides a clear view of upcoming payouts, completed payments, and commissions not yet payable due to refund periods or other factors.
- **Automated Filtering:** Filters based on payment status and method allow you to easily identify commissions ready for payout and manage them effectively.
- **Bulk Actions:** The ability to select multiple payouts for marking as paid with a checkbox simplifies the process and saves time.
- **Export for Mass Payouts:** The "PayPal export" function allows you to generate a file compatible with PayPal for efficient mass payments to your affiliates. This saves you time from manually processing individual payments through PayPal.

### Benefits of Streamlined Payouts:

- **Improved Efficiency:** Bulk actions and data export significantly reduce the time and effort required for processing affiliate payouts.
- **Reduced Errors:** Automated features minimize the risk of errors associated with manual data entry during mass payments.
- **Faster Affiliate Payments:** Efficient payout processing ensures that your affiliates receive their commissions promptly, fostering trust and program satisfaction.

### Additional Considerations:

- **Multiple Payment Methods:** If you offer various payout methods, ensure the "Payments" section allows you to filter and manage payouts based on the chosen method.
- **Payment Receipts:** Generate and provide affiliates with payment receipts for each commission payout to maintain transparency.
- **Payment Schedule Reminders:** Consider setting up automated reminders to ensure timely processing of payouts based on your established schedule.

### Pro Tip: Integrate with Payment Gateways

Explore integrating your affiliate management system with popular payment gateways like PayPal. This can further streamline the payout process and reduce manual intervention.

By effectively utilizing the functionalities within the "Payments" section, you can ensure timely and efficient affiliate payouts, a crucial aspect of maintaining a thriving affiliate program for your online school.

# NETWORK

Building a strong affiliate network takes time and effort, but the long-term benefits are undeniable.

Here's a breakdown of the key points you mentioned and some additional considerations for cultivating a successful program:

**The Power of Affiliates:**

•**Amplified Reach:** Affiliates extend your marketing reach by promoting your courses to their established audiences, driving significant traffic, leads, and sales.

•**Reduced Workload:** Effective affiliate programs lessen your direct marketing efforts, allowing you to focus on course creation and other core aspects of your online school.

•**Brand Advocacy:** Affiliates who genuinely believe in your courses act as brand ambassadors, increasing brand awareness and trust among their audience.

**Building Your Affiliate Network:**

•**Target Audience Alignment:** Identify and recruit affiliates who cater to audiences with an interest in your courses and a propensity to purchase.

•**Value Proposition:** Clearly communicate the benefits of joining your program, highlighting commission structures, marketing materials, and ongoing support.

•**Multiple Recruitment Channels:** Utilize various channels like social media, email marketing, and industry forums to reach potential affiliates.

**Optimizing Your Program:**

•**Performance Tracking:** Monitor affiliate performance data to identify top performers and optimize recruitment strategies accordingly.

•**Incentives and Rewards:** Offer attractive commission structures, bonuses, and rewards to incentivize affiliate promotion efforts.

•**Communication and Support:** Maintain open communication with affiliates, provide necessary resources, and address their concerns promptly.

**Additional Considerations:**

•**Affiliate Program Agreement:** Establish a clear and comprehensive agreement outlining program terms, commission structures, and expectations for both parties.

•**Affiliate Training:** Provide training materials or resources to equip your affiliates with the knowledge and tools they need to effectively promote your courses.

•**Affiliate Tracking:** Implement a reliable affiliate tracking system to accurately monitor clicks, conversions, and commission attribution.

**Remember:** Building a successful affiliate network is an ongoing process. By focusing on audience alignment, value proposition, and program optimization, you can cultivate a team of motivated affiliates who contribute significantly to the growth of your online school.

Quality over quantity is a crucial principle when building your affiliate network. Here's why focusing on qualified affiliates is essential for your online school's program success:

**Prioritizing Quality Affiliates:**

•**Targeted Audience Reach:** Qualified affiliates have established audiences that demonstrably align with your ideal customer profile.

•**Effective Promotions:** Affiliates with relevant expertise and experience know how to effectively promote your courses to their audience, leading to higher conversion rates.

•**Brand Reputation:** Partnering with high-quality affiliates protects your brand reputation and ensures that your courses are promoted in a professional and trustworthy manner.

**Quantity vs. Quality:**

•**Focus on Relevance:** Don't be tempted to prioritize a large number of affiliates if they don't have a relevant audience or proven track record in promoting similar products.

•**Long-Term Benefits:** Investing time in recruiting qualified affiliates generates sustainable growth and higher returns in the long run compared to a large network of underperforming affiliates.

**Identifying Qualified Affiliates:**

•**Audience Analysis:** Look for affiliates who cater to audiences with a demonstrated interest in your course topics and the problems your courses solve.

•**Engagement Metrics:** Consider factors like audience size, engagement levels, and past promotional success when evaluating potential affiliates.

•**Content and Expertise:** Evaluate the content affiliates create and their expertise in your niche to gauge their ability to effectively promote your courses.

**Additional Considerations:**

•**Niche Alignment:** Seek affiliates who specialize in a niche that overlaps with your target audience, ensuring a natural fit for your courses.

•**Affiliate Reviews and Ratings:** Check affiliate reviews and ratings from other businesses or programs to assess their reputation and performance.

•**Communication and Transparency:** Prioritize affiliates who value clear communication and demonstrate a commitment to transparency in their promotional activities.

By focusing on quality over quantity in your affiliate recruitment efforts, you can build a network of partners who are genuinely invested in promoting your online school's courses. This leads to a higher return on investment (ROI) for your program and sustainable growth for your business.

You're absolutely right! These are all fantastic qualities to look for when identifying ideal affiliates for your online school's program. Let's break down each point and explore some additional considerations:

## Essential Affiliate Qualities:

•**Genuine Belief in Course Value:** Affiliates who truly believe in the benefits your courses offer will be more passionate and persuasive in their promotions.

•**Targeted Audience Match:** Their audience should demonstrate a clear interest in the topics or problems addressed by your courses, maximizing conversion potential.

•**Consistent Website Traffic:** A steady flow of qualified traffic to their website indicates an engaged audience receptive to affiliate promotions.

•**Large Email List and Social Following:** A sizeable and active email list and social media following provide valuable channels for affiliates to reach potential customers for your courses.

•**Enthusiasm and Commitment:** Look for affiliates who are genuinely excited about promoting your work and demonstrate a commitment to achieving positive results.

•**Honest Reviews and Endorsements:** Positive and transparent reviews and endorsements from affiliates build trust with potential students and enhance your courses' credibility.

•**Compatible Work Ethic:** Align yourself with affiliates who share a similar work ethic and approach to marketing to ensure a smooth and productive partnership.

•**Affiliate Marketing Experience:** Prior experience in affiliate marketing is certainly a plus, but a strong commitment to learning quickly can also be valuable.

•**Active Course Promotion:** Ideally, affiliates should promote your courses with the same level of effort and creativity they use for their own products.

## Additional Considerations:

•**Content Creation Skills:** Affiliates who excel at creating engaging content, like blog posts, videos, or social media updates, are highly valuable for promoting your courses.

•**Data-Driven Approach:** Look for affiliates who are comfortable analyzing data and optimizing their promotional strategies for better results.

•**Transparency and Compliance:** Prioritize affiliates who understand and adhere to transparency and disclosure guidelines when promoting your courses.

•**Long-Term Partnership Potential:** Seek affiliates who are interested in building a long-term partnership and consistently promoting your courses as your online school grows.

By keeping these qualities in mind, you can recruit a team of high-performing affiliates who contribute significantly to the success of your affiliate marketing program. Remember, quality over quantity is key when building a sustainable and profitable affiliate network.

Your existing network can be a valuable resource for finding potential affiliates for your online school's

program. Here's a breakdown of your observations and some additional strategies to leverage your

network effectively:

## Leveraging Your Existing Network:

•**Expertise and Interest Alignment:** Your professional network likely holds individuals with expertise and interest in your field, making them good candidates to learn about your courses and potentially promote them.

•**Building Upon Existing Relationships:** Leveraging existing connections can be easier than starting from scratch, fostering trust and a foundation for a successful affiliate partnership.

•**Identifying Potential from Within:** Evaluate your network for individuals who may not have extensive affiliate marketing experience but demonstrate qualities like audience alignment and enthusiasm for your courses.

## Strategies for Effective Network Leverage:

•**Targeted Communication:** Reach out to relevant individuals in your network, highlighting the value your courses offer their audience and the benefits of joining your affiliate program.

•**Educational Resources:** Provide training materials or resources to equip those in your network with the knowledge and tools needed to effectively promote your courses.

•**Mentorship and Support:** Offer ongoing mentorship and support to help network affiliates who are new to affiliate marketing and ensure their success in your program.

## Expanding Your Network:

- **LinkedIn Utilization:** Utilize LinkedIn to connect with other entrepreneurs and professionals in your field, potentially finding valuable affiliate partners.
- **Industry Events:** Attend industry events, conferences, and workshops to build your network and connect with potential affiliates.
- **Online Communities:** Engage in online communities relevant to your niche and build relationships with individuals who might be interested in promoting your courses.

**Additional Considerations:**

- **Incentives and Rewards:** Consider offering attractive commission structures or additional incentives to motivate network affiliates who might be starting out in affiliate marketing.
- **Affiliate Program Benefits:** Clearly communicate the benefits of joining your program, emphasizing factors like ongoing support, marketing materials, and transparent commission structures.
- **Track and Analyze Performance:** Monitor the performance of affiliates recruited from your network and adjust your approach accordingly.

**Remember:** Building a successful affiliate network is a continuous process. By leveraging your existing connections, actively expanding your network, and providing support to new affiliates, you can cultivate a valuable team that fuels the growth of your online school.

You're absolutely right! Your students are a fantastic starting point for building your affiliate network. Here's why your students make excellent potential affiliates and some additional considerations for approaching them:

### The Ideal Affiliate: Your Students

- **Credibility and Trust:** Students who have successfully completed your courses and achieved results hold significant credibility and can build trust among potential new students.

- **Passionate Advocates:** Students who genuinely enjoyed your courses and benefited from them are more likely to be passionate advocates for your brand and promote your offerings enthusiastically.

- **Understanding of Course Value:** They possess firsthand knowledge of the value and benefits your courses provide, allowing them to speak authentically to potential customers.

### Benefits of Recruiting Students:

- **Reduced Educational Effort:** Students already understand your courses and teaching style, minimizing the need for extensive training or explanation.

- **Targeted Audience Reach:** They likely have connections to individuals who share similar interests and needs, promoting your courses to a relevant audience.

- **Building Long-Term Relationships:** Recruiting students fosters a win-win scenario, allowing you to generate income while rewarding satisfied customers with commission opportunities.

### Approaching Your Students:

- **Targeted Communication:** Segment your student base and craft targeted messages highlighting the benefits of joining your affiliate program, considering their course completion stage and achievements.

- **Incentives and Rewards:** Offer attractive commission structures, bonuses for successful referrals, or early access to new courses to incentivize student participation in your affiliate program.

- **Transparency and Support:** Provide clear program information, training materials, marketing assets, and ongoing support to empower your student affiliates to succeed.

  **Additional Considerations:**

- **Student Success Stories:** Showcase success stories of students who have benefited from your courses and are now thriving affiliates, inspiring others to join the program.

- **Student Testimonials:** Feature testimonials from satisfied students on your affiliate program page to build trust and credibility for potential new affiliates.

- **Dedicated Affiliate Resources:** Create a dedicated resource section within your affiliate program platform specifically catering to student affiliates, providing them with the tools and support they need. By strategically approaching your students and cultivating a strong affiliate program, you can leverage their positive experiences to fuel the growth of your online school and create a win-win situation for everyone involved.

You're absolutely correct! Targeting niche authorities is a fantastic strategy for attracting high-quality affiliates to your online school's affiliate program. Here's a breakdown of the benefits and some additional considerations for building relationships with niche authorities:

**Niche Authorities: A Valuable Asset**

- **Credibility and Influence:** Niche authorities hold significant influence within their audience and their recommendations carry substantial weight, leading to higher conversion rates for your courses.

- **Targeted Reach:** By partnering with authorities in your niche, you gain access to a highly relevant audience already interested in the topics your courses address.

- **Long-Term Traffic Potential:** Building relationships with niche authorities fosters a foundation for long-term collaboration and sustained traffic generation to your online school.

**Building Relationships with Niche Authorities:**

- **Content Collaboration:** Explore co-creating valuable content, like guest blog posts, webinars, or interviews, to showcase your expertise and establish a connection with the authority's audience.

- **Mutual Promotion:** Offer opportunities for cross-promotion, where you promote the authority's content or products to your audience, and they promote your courses to theirs.

- **Valuable Insights:** Engage with niche authorities by offering your expertise or feedback on their content, demonstrating your knowledge and building rapport.

  **Additional Considerations:**

- **Identify Relevant Authorities:** Research and identify prominent figures and influencers within your specific niche who resonate with your target audience.

- **Value-Added Approach:** Focus on providing value to niche authorities before directly promoting your affiliate program. Build trust and demonstrate your expertise.
- **Respect Their Time:** Be mindful of their busy schedules. Craft concise and compelling communication that highlights the mutual benefits of collaboration.
- **Transparency and Incentives:** Present your affiliate program information transparently and offer attractive commission structures and incentives to entice niche authorities to join.

### Pro Tip: Leverage Social Proof

Showcase testimonials or case studies from existing successful niche authority affiliates on your program's website. This social proof can significantly increase the appeal of your program to other potential high-quality affiliates.

By cultivating relationships with niche authorities and showcasing the value proposition of your affiliate program, you can attract highly influential partners who drive significant traffic and sales for your online school.

That's a great strategy for finding relevant blogs in your niche! Here are some additional tips to refine your search and maximize your results:

- **Targeted Keywords:** Beyond just "[your industry] and 'blog'", incorporate specific keywords related to your niche and the topics you cover in your online courses. This will lead you to blogs with a more focused audience potentially interested in your affiliate program.
- **Search Operators:** Utilize Google search operators to further refine your search. For example, you can use quotation marks (" ") to search for exact phrases or use the minus sign (-) to exclude irrelevant terms.
- **Advanced Search Options:** Explore Google's advanced search options to filter results by date, language, or even specific websites.

### Beyond Blogs:

- **Industry Publications:** Look for industry publications, online magazines, or news websites relevant to your niche. These platforms often feature articles written by niche authorities and can be valuable resources for identifying potential affiliates.
- **Social Media Groups:** Join social media groups and communities focused on your industry. Engaging in discussions and demonstrating your expertise can help you connect with potential affiliates.
- **Podcast Directories:** Search podcast directories for podcasts relevant to your niche. Hosts and guests on these podcasts can be good affiliate partners, especially if they have a loyal audience.

**Remember:** The key is to target platforms and communities where your ideal audience gathers and where potential affiliates are actively building their online presence.

By using a combination of search techniques and exploring various online avenues, you can effectively identify high-quality affiliates who can significantly contribute to the success of your online school's affiliate program.

Social media platforms offer a fantastic way to connect with potential affiliates for your online school's affiliate program. Here's a breakdown of the valuable tools you mentioned and some additional considerations for effective social media exploration:

**Social Media for Affiliate Recruitment:**

- **Facebook Groups:** Join Facebook groups relevant to your niche. Participate in discussions, share your expertise, and subtly introduce your affiliate program when appropriate.
- **LinkedIn Groups:** Engage in LinkedIn groups focused on your industry. Build your professional network, connect with niche authorities, and explore opportunities for collaboration within your affiliate program.
- **Pinterest Boards:** Utilize Pinterest's visual search functionality to discover boards related to your niche topics. Identify individuals who curate content relevant to your courses and consider reaching out to them about potential affiliate partnerships.

**Additional Social Media Strategies:**

- **Content Sharing:** Share valuable content related to your courses on social media platforms to attract potential affiliates interested in promoting such content to their audience.
- **Targeted Ads:** Consider running targeted social media ad campaigns to reach a wider audience of potential affiliates within your niche.
- **Influencer Marketing:** Identify social media influencers in your niche with a strong and engaged following. Explore opportunities for collaboration and potential affiliate partnerships.

**General Social Media Tips:**

- **Authentic Engagement:** Focus on building genuine connections and providing value within social media communities. Avoid solely promoting your affiliate program.
- **Transparency and Disclosure:** Always be transparent and disclose your affiliate relationships whenever promoting courses through social media channels.
- **Track and Analyze:** Monitor the performance of your social media outreach efforts and adjust your strategies for optimal results in attracting potential affiliates.

**Remember:** Social media provides a powerful platform for networking, building relationships, and identifying potential affiliates. By utilizing these platforms strategically, you can connect with a wider audience of partners who can significantly contribute to your affiliate program's success.

Affiliate marketing networks are a fantastic way to find groups of affiliate marketers who can be potential partners for your online school's program. Here's a breakdown of the benefits and some additional considerations for leveraging affiliate networks:

### Affiliate Marketing Networks: A Hub for Collaboration

- **Vast Affiliate Pool:** Affiliate networks connect you with a vast pool of potential affiliate partners, increasing your chances of finding high-quality affiliates who align with your target audience.
- **Program Management Tools:** Many networks provide tools to manage your affiliate program efficiently, including tracking performance, processing payouts, and communicating with affiliates.
- **Networking Opportunities:** Networks often host online forums or communities where you can connect with other affiliate marketers and program managers, fostering valuable knowledge exchange and potential partnerships.

diggitymarketing.com

Affiliate marketing networks

### Additional Considerations:

- **Network Selection:** Carefully research and select affiliate networks that cater to your niche and target audience. Consider factors like network size, fees, and available program management tools.
- **Affiliate Profiles:** Review affiliate profiles within the network to identify potential partners who demonstrate the qualities you're looking for, such as audience relevance, promotional experience, and a track record of success.
- **Network Engagement:** Actively participate in network forums and communities. Share valuable insights, connect with potential affiliates, and build relationships within the affiliate marketing ecosystem.

### Pro Tip: Leverage Network Expertise

Many affiliate networks offer educational resources and support services to help you navigate affiliate marketing and optimize your program for success. Take advantage of these resources to gain valuable insights and maximize the benefits of utilizing affiliate networks.

By joining relevant affiliate marketing networks and actively engaging with the community, you can significantly expand your reach and connect with a wider pool of qualified affiliate partners who can propel your online school's program to new heights.

Once you've identified potential affiliates who are interested in your brand, building a personal connection is crucial for establishing a successful partnership. Here's a breakdown of the importance of avoiding cold emails and some alternative strategies for reaching out:

### Why Avoid Cold Emails?

- **Low Response Rates:** Cold emails often land in spam folders and generate low response rates, hindering your efforts to connect with potential affiliates.

- **Lack of Personalization:** Generic emails don't resonate with recipients and fail to establish a rapport, making them less likely to consider your offer.

- **Negative Perception:** Cold emails can come across as impersonal and pushy, potentially damaging your brand image and creating a negative first impression.

### Effective Outreach Strategies:

- **Warm Introductions:** Leverage your existing network to seek introductions to potential affiliates. A trusted connection can vouch for you and significantly improve your chances of getting a positive response.

- **Targeted Communication:** Craft personalized messages that highlight the affiliate's specific audience relevance and the potential benefits of joining your program. Showcase success stories of existing affiliates in their niche to demonstrate program value.

- **Value Proposition Focus:** Focus your outreach on the value proposition for the potential affiliate. Explain how your program can benefit them and their audience, emphasizing attractive commission structures, marketing materials, and ongoing support.

- **Social Media Engagement:** Engage with potential affiliates on social media platforms. Respond to their comments, share valuable content, and build relationships before directly introducing your affiliate program.

### Crafting a Compelling Introduction:

- **Start with a Strong Opener:** Personalize the introduction by mentioning something specific about the potential affiliate's work or recent achievements.

- **Highlight Shared Interests:** Demonstrate that you've researched their niche and identify areas of shared interest to establish a connection.

- **Offer Value First:** Before proposing the affiliate program, offer something valuable, like a free course sample or exclusive content relevant to their audience.

- **Clear Call to Action:** End your message with a clear call to action, inviting them to learn more about your program or schedule a call to discuss further.

**Remember:** Building relationships is key. By focusing on personalized outreach, value proposition, and genuine connection, you can attract high-quality affiliates who are genuinely interested in promoting your online school's courses.

## COMPETITION

In a crowded affiliate marketing landscape, crafting a compelling program and standing out is crucial for attracting high-quality affiliates to your online school.

Here's a breakdown of the key points you mentioned and some additional considerations for creating a program that attracts top affiliates:

### Standing Out in the Affiliate Marketplace:

- **Program Competitiveness:** Analyze your competitors' affiliate programs to identify their strengths and weaknesses. Design your program to offer more favorable commission structures, valuable marketing materials, or additional benefits that entice affiliates.

- **Value Proposition Clarity:** Clearly articulate the value proposition for potential affiliates. Emphasize high commission rates, timely payouts, a user-friendly tracking system, and ongoing support to ensure their success.

- **Quality Course Content:** The foundation of your program lies in the quality and value of your online courses. Ensure your courses are well-designed, informative, and deliver genuine results for students, which affiliates can confidently promote.

### Optimizing Your Affiliate Program:

- **Attractive Commission Structures:** Offer competitive commission rates or tiered structures that incentivize affiliates to actively promote your courses.

- **High-Converting Marketing Materials:** Provide affiliates with professional and high-converting marketing materials like banners, landing pages, or email templates to make their job easier.

- **Reliable Tracking and Reporting:** Implement a robust tracking and reporting system that allows affiliates to monitor their performance and earnings transparently.

- **Prompt Payouts:** Ensure timely and reliable payouts to affiliates to maintain trust and motivate them to continue promoting your courses.

- **Ongoing Communication and Support:** Maintain open and regular communication with your affiliates. Address their concerns promptly, offer ongoing support, and provide valuable resources to help them succeed.

### Building a Strong Affiliate Network:

- **Focus on Quality over Quantity:** Prioritize attracting high-quality affiliates who align with your target audience and demonstrate a proven track record in promoting similar products.

- **Niche Targeting:** Tailor your program's benefits and communication to specific affiliate niches to attract partners with a relevant audience.

- **Incentivize Referrals:** Offer bonus structures or rewards to encourage existing affiliates to refer other qualified partners to your program.

- **Promote Affiliate Success Stories:** Showcase success stories of top-performing affiliates to inspire others and demonstrate the program's earning potential.

**Remember:** Building a successful affiliate program is an ongoing process. By continually optimizing your program, providing value to affiliates, and fostering a supportive partnership environment, you can attract and retain top-tier affiliates who contribute significantly to the growth of your online school.

When it comes to affiliate marketing for your online school, staying focused on a niche market is crucial for success. Here's a breakdown of why niche targeting is essential and some additional considerations for refining your approach:

### The Power of Niche Marketing in Affiliate Marketing:

- **Targeted Audience:** A well-defined niche allows you to target affiliates who cater to a specific audience with a demonstrably high interest in your courses, leading to better conversion rates.

- **Credibility and Authority:** Focusing on a niche helps you establish yourself as an authority in that specific area. Affiliates can then confidently promote your courses knowing they cater to a well-defined audience need.

- **Effective Communication:** Niche targeting allows you to tailor your communication and marketing materials to resonate more effectively with both affiliates and their audience.

### Examples of Profitable Niches:

- You mentioned several great examples, including fine arts, music, fitness (gym & pilates), gardening, dancing, and DIY & knitting. These are all viable niches with passionate audiences who might be interested in online courses to learn new skills or deepen their knowledge.

### Additional Considerations:

- **Niche Research and Selection:** Conduct thorough research to identify a profitable niche that aligns with your expertise and course offerings. Consider factors like market size, competition level, and affiliate program saturation within the niche.

- **Going Hyper-Niche:** Within your chosen niche, consider exploring even more specific sub-niches. For example, within "fitness," you could target pilates for beginners or yoga for athletes.

- **Long-Term Growth:** While a hyper-niche approach can be effective, plan for potential growth within your chosen niche. Consider offering a variety of courses that cater to different skill levels or interests within the broader niche.

**Remember:** Niche marketing is not about limiting your reach; it's about targeting the right audience. By focusing on a well-defined niche, you can attract high-quality affiliates with relevant audiences, leading to increased sales and a thriving affiliate program for your online school.

Offering a free course or trial is a fantastic strategy for attracting potential affiliates to your online school's affiliate program. Here's a breakdown of the benefits and some additional considerations for implementing this approach:

## The Value of Free Courses and Trials for Affiliate Recruitment:

- **Reduced Risk and Increased Trust:** By offering a free course or trial, you allow potential affiliates to experience the quality and value of your content firsthand, reducing their perceived risk and fostering trust in your program.

- **Informed Promotion:** Affiliates who have experienced your courses can confidently promote them to their audience, speaking from a place of knowledge and genuine enthusiasm.

- **Improved Conversion Rates:** When affiliates understand the benefits your courses offer, they can create more targeted and persuasive promotions, leading to higher conversion rates for your program.

### Leveraging Affiliate Marketplaces:
- **Vast Affiliate Pool:** Affiliate marketplaces connect you with a large pool of potential affiliates actively seeking products or services to promote. This broadens your reach and increases your chances of finding high-quality partners.
- **Program Visibility:** Listing your program on reputable marketplaces increases its visibility within the affiliate marketing community, attracting affiliates who might not have found you otherwise.
- **Streamlined Management:** Some marketplaces offer tools for managing your affiliate program, including tracking performance, processing payouts, and communicating with affiliates.

### Examples of Popular Affiliate Marketplaces:
- You've mentioned several great options, including JVZoo, Zaxaa, PayDotCom, ShareASale, e-Junkie, and ClickBank. These platforms cater to a wide range of industries and offer different features and functionalities.

### Additional Considerations:
- **Marketplace Selection:** Research and compare different affiliate marketplaces to find one that aligns with your niche, target audience, and budget. Consider factors like platform fees, available features, and the types of affiliates typically active on each marketplace.
- **Program Presentation:** Craft a compelling program description on the marketplace that highlights your value proposition, commission rates, and the benefits affiliates can expect from partnering with you.
- **Application Requirements:** Review the application requirements for each marketplace and ensure your program meets their criteria. Some marketplaces might have minimum traffic requirements or product quality standards.
- **Transparency and Honesty:** As you mentioned, be transparent and honest in your program listing. Clearly outline commission structures, payout terms, and any other relevant details to build trust with potential affiliates.

### Beyond Marketplaces:
- Remember, affiliate marketplaces are just one avenue for finding affiliates. Consider using a combination of strategies, including social media outreach, networking within your niche, and offering valuable content to attract potential partners.

By effectively utilizing affiliate marketplaces and implementing a comprehensive outreach strategy, you can significantly expand your network of potential affiliates and fuel the growth of your online school's affiliate program.

# SEO

That's a great point! SEO is a crucial element for affiliate marketing success, and ongoing keyword research and a clear strategy are essential. Here's a breakdown of your insights and some additional tips for affiliate marketing SEO:

### Keyword Research: A Continuous Process

- **Regular Monitoring:** You're absolutely right. Keyword demand and competition levels fluctuate. Regularly revisit your keyword research to identify new opportunities and ensure your targeting remains effective.

- **Keyword Mix:** Balance popular, competitive keywords with targeted, high-intent keywords. Popular keywords attract broader traffic, while high-intent keywords convert better because they indicate strong purchase intent.

### Maintaining SEO and Affiliate Program Harmony:

- **Content Strategy Alignment:** Ensure your SEO content strategy aligns seamlessly with your affiliate program. Content should inform, educate, and naturally integrate product recommendations without being overly promotional.

- **Transparency and Communication:** Maintain clear communication with affiliate partners. Share your SEO strategy and content calendar to avoid any potential conflicts or confusion.

### Additional SEO Tips for Affiliate Marketers:

- **Optimize Your Affiliate Landing Pages:** Ensure affiliate landing pages are optimized for relevant keywords, include high-quality visuals, and provide a clear call to action for visitors to convert.

- **Internal Linking:** Strategically link to your affiliate partners' pages from relevant content within your website. This improves navigation for visitors and increases traffic to affiliate products.

- **Mobile-Friendliness:** Make sure your website and affiliate landing pages are mobile-friendly, as a significant portion of online traffic comes from mobile devices.

**Remember:** SEO is a long-term strategy. By continuously refining your keyword research, maintaining alignment with your affiliate program, and implementing these additional tips, you can leverage SEO to attract qualified traffic and drive sales through your affiliate partnerships.

Here's a breakdown of the potential conflicts that can arise between your SEO efforts and your affiliate program, along with strategies to ensure a harmonious partnership:

### Avoiding Keyword Cannibalization with Affiliates:

- **Transparency and Communication:** As you mentioned, clear communication is key. At the program's outset, discuss keyword targeting strategies with affiliates. Clearly outline any terms you don't want them to bid on, such as your brand name or specific course titles.
- **Targeted Keyword Strategies:** Encourage affiliates to focus on promoting your courses using long-tail keywords related to your niche and target audience. This helps attract qualified leads while minimizing competition for core keywords.
- **Content Collaboration:** Consider collaborating with affiliates on content creation. Guest blog posts or co-created resources can leverage each other's SEO strengths and reach without direct competition.
- **Focus on Value Proposition:** Emphasize the value proposition for affiliates beyond just organic search traffic. Highlight additional promotional methods like social media marketing or email marketing to diversify their efforts.

### Maintaining Open Communication:

- **Regular Check-Ins:** Schedule regular meetings or calls with your affiliates to discuss performance, share industry insights, and address any SEO-related concerns.
- **Open Communication Channels:** Establish clear communication channels where affiliates can reach out with questions, concerns, or suggestions regarding SEO and keyword targeting.

### The Importance of SEO for Online Schools:

You're right, SEO is crucial for online schools. It allows potential students to discover your courses organically through search engines. By implementing a strong SEO strategy, you can:

- **Improve Brand Visibility:** Rank higher in search engine results pages (SERPs) for relevant keywords, increasing brand awareness and attracting organic traffic.
- **Target Ideal Students:** Attract qualified leads who are actively searching for courses like yours, leading to higher conversion rates and student enrollment.
- **Establish Authority:** Strong SEO demonstrates your expertise in your niche and positions your online

school as a credible and valuable resource for potential students.

By addressing potential SEO conflicts, maintaining open communication with affiliates, and leveraging SEO for your online school, you can foster a thriving affiliate program that complements your organic traffic generation efforts.

## PARTNERSHIP

You're absolutely right! A successful affiliate program thrives on a balanced give-and-take relationship between you and your affiliate partners. Here's a breakdown of this key concept and some additional thoughts on fostering a mutually beneficial partnership:

**The Give-and-Take Dynamic in Affiliate Marketing:**

- **Value Proposition for Affiliates:** At the program's core lies a compelling value proposition for your affiliates. This includes attractive commission rates, timely payouts, high-converting marketing materials, and ongoing support to ensure their success.

- **High-Quality Courses:** The foundation of the equation is your online course itself. It needs to be well-designed, informative, and deliver genuine results for students, which affiliates can confidently promote.

- **Multi-Channel Promotion:** Ideally, your affiliates promote your courses across various channels, such as their websites, social media platforms, email marketing campaigns, or even offline methods if relevant to your niche.

**Building a Strong Affiliate Network:**

- **Focus on Quality over Quantity:** Prioritize attracting high-quality affiliates with a proven track record, a relevant audience, and a genuine interest in promoting your courses.

- **Niche Targeting:** Tailor your program and communication to specific affiliate niches to attract partners with a well-matched audience.

- **Ongoing Communication and Support:** Maintain open and regular communication with your affiliates. Be responsive to their questions, offer ongoing support, and provide valuable resources to help them succeed.

- **Incentivize Success:** Implement reward structures or bonus programs to motivate affiliates and encourage continued promotion of your courses.

- **Track and Analyze Performance:** Monitor the performance of your affiliate program and individual affiliates. Use data insights to identify opportunities for improvement and optimize your program for better results.

**Reaching the Perfect Balance:**

By providing excellent courses (your give) and empowering your affiliates with the tools and resources they need to succeed (your take), you can cultivate a win-win partnership. This fosters a strong and supportive affiliate network that drives significant growth and sales for your online school.

Providing affiliates with informative materials and tools is essential for their success, which ultimately translates to your success. Here's a breakdown of the importance of offering these resources and some additional tips for maximizing their impact:

**Empowering Affiliates with Valuable Resources:**

- **Enhanced Understanding:** Equipping affiliates with comprehensive information about your online school, courses, target audience, and value proposition allows them to grasp the product's essence and promote it more effectively.

- **Improved Credibility:** When affiliates possess in-depth knowledge about your courses, they can confidently answer potential student inquiries and build trust with their audience.
- **Effective Promotion:** The resources you provide can be instrumental in crafting compelling marketing materials and messages that resonate with the affiliate's audience and drive conversions.

**Examples of Informative Materials and Tools:**

- **Course Descriptions and Reviews:** Provide detailed descriptions of your courses, including learning objectives, target audience, instructor profiles, and student testimonials.
- **Marketing Materials:** Equip affiliates with a variety of marketing materials, such as banners, social media graphics, email templates, and promotional copy, to save them time and effort.
- **Affiliate Dashboard:** Offer a user-friendly affiliate dashboard where affiliates can access real-time performance data, track their earnings, and download marketing materials.
- **Case Studies and Success Stories:** Share success stories of students who have benefited from your courses. This social proof can be powerful in convincing potential students to enroll.

**Additional Tips for Effective Resource Delivery:**

- **Multiple Formats:** Provide resources in various formats, such as text documents, video tutorials, or infographics, to cater to different learning preferences.
- **Regular Updates:** Keep your resource library updated with the latest course information, marketing materials, and industry trends.
- **Accessibility:** Ensure all resources are easily accessible within your affiliate program portal or a dedicated resource library.
- **Communication and Support:** Offer clear instructions on how to use the resources effectively and provide ongoing support to answer any questions affiliates might have.

By providing informative materials, empowering your affiliates with valuable tools, and fostering open communication, you can equip them for success. This translates into a stronger affiliate network that significantly contributes to your online school's growth.

**Timely commission payouts are crucial for building trust and maintaining a healthy relationship with your affiliate partners. Here's a breakdown of the importance of prompt payments and some additional considerations for managing affiliate commissions**

effectively:

### The Importance of Timely Commission Payouts:
•**Trust and Partnership:** Promptly paying commissions demonstrates your reliability and strengthens the trust between you and your affiliates. This fosters a positive partnership environment where everyone feels valued.
•**Motivation and Performance:** Knowing they'll be paid on time motivates affiliates to continue promoting your courses diligently. This can lead to increased sales and a thriving affiliate program.
•**Affiliate Satisfaction:** Reliable and timely payouts contribute significantly to affiliate satisfaction. Satisfied affiliates are more likely to remain active partners and continue promoting your online school in the long run.

### Optimizing Your Affiliate Commission Management:
•**Clear Payment Schedule:** Outline a clear and consistent payment schedule within your affiliate program agreement. Specify the exact date or timeframe affiliates can expect to receive their commissions.
•**Transparent Payment Methods:** Offer a variety of convenient and reliable payment methods for affiliates to receive their commissions, such as PayPal, wire transfer, or direct deposit.
•**Automated Payouts:** Consider implementing an automated payout system to ensure timely and efficient commission distribution, minimizing manual work and potential delays.
•**Accurate Tracking and Reporting:** Maintain accurate records of affiliate earnings and commission rates. Provide affiliates with transparent reporting tools to track their performance and commission accrual.
•**Open Communication:** Maintain open communication with affiliates regarding commission payments. Address any questions or concerns promptly to avoid misunderstandings.

### Building Long-Term Partnerships:
By prioritizing timely commission payouts, you demonstrate your commitment to a successful partnership. This builds trust, motivates your affiliates, and fosters a collaborative environment that fuels the growth of your online school's affiliate program.

Building strong relationships is fundamental to success in affiliate marketing, especially with your partners. Here's a breakdown of the importance of relationship building and some additional tips for fostering a collaborative environment:

### The Power of Relationships in Affiliate Marketing:

- **Mutual Benefit:** Affiliate marketing thrives on a win-win situation. By building strong relationships, you foster open communication and collaboration, allowing both you and your affiliates to work towards shared goals and achieve mutual success.

- **Understanding Partner Needs:** Taking the time to understand your affiliates' backgrounds, target audience, and marketing strengths allows you to tailor your program and resources to their specific needs. This empowers them to promote your courses more effectively.

- **Long-Term Partnerships:** Strong relationships foster loyalty and trust, leading to long-term partnerships with your affiliates. This translates into consistent promotion of your courses and a reliable source of revenue for your online school.

### Strategies for Building Strong Affiliate Relationships:

- **Get to Know Your Partners:** Before onboarding affiliates, invest time in researching their background, niche expertise, and audience demographics.

- **Personalized Communication:** Avoid a "one-size-fits-all" approach. Personalize your communication with each affiliate, addressing their unique needs and concerns.

- **Regular Communication:** Maintain consistent communication with your affiliates. Schedule regular calls or meetings to discuss performance, industry trends, and potential areas for collaboration.

- **Openness and Transparency:** Be transparent with your affiliates about your program, commission structures, and performance expectations. Encourage open communication and address any concerns promptly.

- **Support and Recognition:** Offer ongoing support to your affiliates and recognize their achievements. This could involve providing valuable resources, celebrating milestones, or offering bonus incentives.

**Building a Collaborative Ecosystem:**

By prioritizing relationship building, fostering open communication, and demonstrating your commitment to their success, you can cultivate a collaborative ecosystem with your affiliates. This environment will drive a thriving affiliate program that fuels the growth of your online school.

Gathering positive reviews from your existing affiliate partners is a powerful marketing strategy for attracting new affiliates to your online school's program. Here's a breakdown of the benefits of affiliate testimonials and some additional considerations for collecting and utilizing them effectively:

**The Value of Affiliate Testimonials:**

- **Social Proof and Credibility:** Positive testimonials from satisfied affiliates serve as social proof, demonstrating the program's effectiveness and building trust with potential partners.

- **Transparency and Authenticity:** Affiliate testimonials provide genuine and transparent insights into the program's benefits, commission structure, and overall experience from a partner's perspective.

- **Increased Appeal and Trust:** Showcasing positive affiliate experiences can significantly increase your program's appeal and build trust with potential partners who are considering joining.

**Strategies for Collecting Effective Affiliate Testimonials:**

- **Direct Requests:** After establishing a positive working relationship, directly request testimonials from your top-performing affiliates.

- **Provide Guidelines:** Offer clear guidelines on what you'd like affiliates to highlight in their testimonials, such as their experience, program benefits, or specific successes they've achieved.

- **Multiple Formats:** Consider collecting testimonials in various formats, such as written text, video reviews, or case studies, to cater to different preferences.

**Utilizing Affiliate Testimonials Effectively:**

- **Dedicated Testimonial Page:** Create a dedicated page on your website showcasing affiliate testimonials. Ensure it's easily accessible to potential partners exploring your program.
- **Social Proof on Landing Pages:** Strategically integrate positive testimonials into your affiliate program landing pages or marketing materials to enhance their persuasive power.
- **Case Studies for High Performers:** Develop in-depth case studies highlighting the achievements of your top-performing affiliates. This showcases the program's earning potential and motivates new partners.
- **Social Media Promotion:** Share positive affiliate testimonials on social media platforms to increase visibility and reach a wider audience of potential partners.

**Building Trust and Transparency:**

Remember, authenticity is key. Encourage honest feedback from your affiliates, even if it includes constructive criticism. Addressing any concerns demonstrates transparency and a willingness to improve your program, ultimately fostering trust with potential partners.

By actively collecting and showcasing positive affiliate testimonials, you can leverage social proof and build trust with potential partners. This can significantly enhance the appeal of your program and attract high-quality affiliates who contribute to the continued success of your online school.

Introducing contests and gamification elements can be a fantastic way to boost engagement and incentivize your affiliate partners. Here's a breakdown of the benefits of contests for affiliates and some additional considerations for implementing them effectively:

**The Power of Affiliate Contests:**

- **Increased Engagement:** Contests can breathe new life into your affiliate program, sparking healthy competition and motivating affiliates to promote your courses more actively.
- **Enhanced Performance:** The prospect of winning a prize can incentivize affiliates to invest more time and effort into promoting your courses, potentially leading to increased sales and program growth.
- **Building Relationships:** Contests can foster a sense of community and camaraderie among your affiliates. They can also provide opportunities for interaction and knowledge sharing.

**Creative Contest Ideas for Affiliates:**

- **Sales Contests:** Reward affiliates who generate the most sales or leads within a specific timeframe.
- **Social Media Engagement Contests:** Recognize affiliates who create the most engaging social media posts promoting your courses.
- **Creative Marketing Contests:** Award prizes for the most unique or effective marketing campaign developed by an affiliate to promote your courses.
- **Referral Contests:** Incentivize affiliates to refer new partners to your program by offering bonuses for

successful referrals.

**Additional Considerations for Affiliate Contests:**

- **Clear Goals and Objectives:** Define clear goals for your contest, such as increasing sales, boosting social media engagement, or attracting new affiliates.

- **Aligned with Program Values:** Ensure your contest prizes and mechanics are aligned with your program's overall value proposition and incentivize the behaviors you value most.

- **Fairness and Transparency:** Establish clear contest rules, eligibility criteria, and a fair judging process to maintain trust with your affiliates.

- **Promote the Contest:** Actively promote your affiliate contest across different channels to ensure all partners are aware and can participate.

- **Measure and Analyze:** Track the results of your contest and analyze its impact on affiliate engagement and program performance. This allows you to refine your approach for future contests.

**Keeping Affiliates Engaged:**

By incorporating contests alongside other engagement strategies like regular communication, valuable resources, and recognition programs, you can create a dynamic and exciting environment for your affiliate partners. This fosters a win-win situation, leading to a thriving affiliate program that fuels the growth of your online school.

Here's a breakdown of the importance of seeking feedback from your affiliates and some additional thoughts on fostering a culture of open communication:

**The Value of Affiliate Feedback:**

•**Identifying Areas for Improvement:** Feedback from your affiliates can reveal blind spots and areas where your program can be improved. This can be anything from commission structures to marketing materials or communication strategies.

•**Enhancing Affiliate Experience:** By actively seeking feedback, you demonstrate your commitment to creating a positive experience for your affiliates. This fosters trust and goodwill and encourages them to provide honest and valuable insights.

•**Retaining Existing Affiliates:** Regularly soliciting feedback allows you to address any concerns or frustrations your affiliates might have. This proactive approach can help retain existing partners and prevent churn within your program.

**Strategies for Encouraging Affiliate Feedback:**

•**Surveys and Questionnaires:** Conduct periodic surveys or questionnaires to gather feedback from your affiliates on various aspects of your program.

•**One-on-One Communication:** Schedule regular calls or meetings with your affiliates to discuss their experience, challenges, and suggestions for improvement.

•**Open Communication Channels:** Establish clear communication channels where affiliates can easily reach out to you with feedback, questions, or concerns.

**Building a Culture of Open Communication:**

•**Value All Feedback:** Make it clear that you value all feedback, both positive and negative. This encourages affiliates to be honest and transparent in their responses.

•**Acknowledge and Respond:** Acknowledge all feedback you receive from your affiliates and demonstrate that you're taking their input seriously. Respond with a plan of action or explanation for how you'll address their suggestions.

- **Continuous Improvement:** Demonstrate a commitment to continuous improvement by implementing the feedback you receive. This shows your affiliates that their voices are heard and valued.

**Attracting New Affiliates:**

By fostering a culture of open communication and actively seeking feedback from your existing affiliates, you demonstrate that you prioritize building a strong and mutually beneficial partnership. This positive reputation can significantly enhance the appeal of your program and attract new high-quality affiliates to your online school.

They can be a valuable tool for driving traffic and conversions, but it's important to be strategic in your approach. Here's a breakdown of the pros and cons of using coupon sites, along with some tips for maximizing their effectiveness:

**The Benefits of Coupon Sites:**

- **Increased Brand Awareness:** Listing your courses on reputable coupon sites can expose your online school to a wider audience actively searching for deals and discounts.

- **Targeted Customer Acquisition:** Coupon sites attract customers who are specifically interested in finding discounts, potentially leading to a higher conversion rate for your courses.

- **Boosted Website Traffic:** By directing affiliates and customers to coupon sites with your offers, you can generate additional website traffic and increase overall visibility.

**The Potential Drawbacks of Coupon Sites:**

- **Reduced Perceived Value:** Offering deep discounts through coupon sites can sometimes lead to a perception of your courses having a lower value.

- **Profit Margin Erosion:** Significant discounts offered through coupon sites can eat into your profit margins, so it's crucial to carefully calculate the cost-effectiveness.

- **Limited Control:** You have less control over how your courses are presented on coupon sites, and the overall user experience might not be optimized for your brand.

**Tips for Using Coupon Sites Effectively:**

- **Selective Targeting:** Partner with high-quality, relevant coupon sites that align with your target audience and brand image.

- **Strategic Discounting:** Offer targeted discounts on specific courses or bundles rather than blanketing your entire program with deep cuts.

- **Track and Analyze Performance:** Monitor the traffic and conversions generated through coupon sites to assess their effectiveness and adjust your strategy accordingly.

- **Clear Communication:** Clearly communicate the terms and conditions of any discounts offered through coupon sites to avoid confusion for potential students.

**Alternative Strategies for Reaching Deal-Seekers:**

- **Limited-Time Promotions:** Consider offering limited-time promotions or early bird discounts directly on your website to attract deal-conscious customers.

- **Value Bundles:** Create attractive value bundles that combine multiple courses at a discounted price, offering a perception of greater value compared to individual discounts.
- **Free Trials or Demos:** Provide potential students with free trial access or introductory course demos to showcase the quality and value of your offerings.

By carefully considering the pros and cons, implementing a strategic approach, and exploring alternative strategies, you can leverage coupon sites effectively to attract new students and grow your online school without sacrificing long-term profitability.

Partnering with key influencers can be a powerful strategy for driving targeted traffic and potential students to your online school. Here's a breakdown of the benefits of influencer marketing and some additional considerations for choosing the right partners:

### The Power of Influencer Marketing:

- **Increased Brand Awareness:** Influencers with established audiences can significantly expand your school's reach and introduce your courses to a wider pool of potential students.
- **Enhanced Credibility:** Endorsements from trusted influencers can add credibility and social proof to your online school, making your courses more appealing to their audience.
- **Targeted Audience Engagement:** By partnering with niche-relevant influencers, you can connect with a highly targeted audience already interested in the subject matter your courses cover.

### Selecting the Right Influencers:

- **Beyond Follower Count:** Look beyond just follower count. Focus on engagement metrics like likes, comments, and shares to gauge genuine audience interaction.
- **Niche Alignment:** Choose influencers whose niche and target audience closely align with your online school's offerings to ensure maximum relevance and impact.
- **Content and Values:** Partner with influencers whose content and values resonate with your brand and the message you want to convey about your online school.
- **Authenticity and Transparency:** Prioritize influencers who are authentic and transparent in their recommendations. Their audience should trust their judgment for genuine course promotion.

### Additional Tips for Successful Influencer Marketing:

- **Clear Goals and Objectives:** Define clear goals for your influencer campaign, such as brand awareness, website traffic, or course enrollments.
- **Collaboration and Content Creation:** Work collaboratively with influencers to develop engaging content that promotes your courses organically within their audience.
- **Track and Analyze Results:** Track the performance of your influencer campaign to measure its

effectiveness and optimize your strategy for future collaborations.

**Alternative Strategies for Reaching Your Target Audience:**

- **Social Media Marketing:** Build a strong social media presence for your online school and engage with your target audience directly.

- **Content Marketing:** Develop valuable and informative content relevant to your courses to attract organic traffic and establish yourself as an authority in your niche.

- **Community Building:** Create online communities or forums where potential students can connect, ask questions, and learn more about your courses.

By carefully selecting the right influencers, developing a strategic campaign, and exploring alternative strategies, you can leverage influencer marketing to effectively reach your target audience and attract new students to your online school.